PRAISE FOR *FEDERATION*

Patrick McMahon Glynn was not the typical nineteenth century Irish immigrant. Erudite and principled, this committed Catholic's contribution to Australian society as a lawyer and parliamentarian has long deserved to be better known. Anne Henderson's compelling and scholarly *Federation's Man of Letters* ably fills this gap.

MARGARET BEAZLEY AO QC

This insightful portrait of one of the founders of our Federation shows him in his political, social, and religious context. An immigrant Irish lawyer, who settled in South Australia, P. M. Glynn took up issues (such as Murray River water rights) which have never lost their relevance. Eulogised by Prime Minister Scullin as "a great scholar and a cultured and eloquent speaker", he is a worthy subject for Anne Henderson's impressive and informative essay.

MURRAY GLEESON AC QC

This biographical study is both delight and revelation. Here was a Federation-era politician on the right side of so many issues, bold enough to advocate humane treatment of the Chinese in the Australian colonies and to urge free-trade rather than protection. As early as 1898 he saw the day when "the centre of the world struggle is being shifted west to east" and England may not be able to protect Australia. He was the one Catholic in the leadership of the non-Labor Parties; by any test as thoughtful and learned a politician as we ever had.

BOB CARR

THE KAPUNDA PRESS

Series editor: *Damien Freeman*

Fellow of the PM Glynn Institute, Australian Catholic University

The Kapunda Press is an imprint of Connor Court Publishing in association with the PM Glynn Institute.

Current titles in this series:

FEDERATION'S MAN OF LETTERS

PATRICK McMAHON GLYNN

ANNE HENDERSON

THE KAPUNDA PRESS

Connor Court Publishing Pty Ltd

Copyright © 2019 as a collection, Damien Freeman; individual chapters, the contributors

PO Box 7257
Redland Bay QLD 4165
sales@connorcourt.com
www.connorcourt.com

ISBN: 9781925826487

Cover design by Ian James

Printed in Australia

Contents

"I spent the day in the Botanical Gardens reading my constant companion Shakespeare."

Patrick McMahon Glynn's diary entry for Christmas Day 1881

Foreword

Gerald O'Collins

By launching the PM Glynn Institute on 13 October 2016, Australian Catholic University established a think-tank to examine challenges facing government, society as a whole, and Christianity in this country. With the admirable Dr Michael Casey as its director, this centre aims to develop research in such areas as education, healthcare, human rights, and immigration, and so be in a position to formulate workable and worthwhile proposals for a healthier and more humane Australian life.

The institute has drawn its name and inspiration from my maternal grandfather, Patrick McMahon Glynn, an Irish barrister who migrated to the self-governing colony of Victoria in 1880 and, two years later, settled in South Australia. He became a South Australian politician, was elected to the federal convention of 1897–98, and played a significant role in drafting the Australian Constitution. Entering the House of Representatives in 1901, he served as a minister in three Commonwealth governments, and his nineteen years as a member made him the last of the Founding Fathers to remain in the national parliament. Melbourne University Press (in association with Cambridge University Press) published in 1965 my biography of Glynn. In 1974, Polding Press (Melbourne) published my edited volume, *Patrick McMahon Glynn: Letters to His Family (1974–1927)*.

Along with my whole family, I was naturally delighted to find ACU choosing my grandfather as an inspirational figure for the name of their new institute. His contribution to the story of Australia has regularly proved of more than antiquarian interest. In the referendum of 6 November 1999, the Australian public voted against becoming a republic with the Queen and Governor-General being replaced by a president. In the same referendum they also rejected a much longer preamble that was meant to replace the brief preamble which Glynn had succeeded in adding as an amendment to the Constitution: "humbly relying on the blessing of Almighty God."

Despite the fact that section 51 of the Constitution did not include religion among the matters for which the federal parliament would be empowered to make laws, Henry Bournes Higgins, a Victorian delegate at the federal convention, who was to become a famous High Court judge, feared, nevertheless, that the reference to God in the preamble could result in some Commonwealth powers over religion being claimed by implication and proposed what now stands as section 116 of the Constitution. Glynn voted for this new clause. His own amendment had looked only to give expression to the basic religious belief of most Australian people.

The meaning of the preamble, section 51 (and the related section 96), and section 116 of the Constitution came under scrutiny when the Council for the Defence of Government Schools (DOGS) brought (and lost) a High Court case against public money going to non-government schools. In August 2017, the Royal Commission into Institutional Responses to Child Sexual Abuse, recommended legislation that would make failure to report relevant information a criminal offence, adding: "We acknowledge that if this recommendation is implemented, then clergy hearing confessions may have to decide between complying with the civil law obligation to report and complying with a duty in their role as confessor." Besides questioning the seal of confession, this proposal appears to be in conflict with section 116 of the Constitution – at least if the proposal is calling for a national law.

The biography of my grandfather contained a chapter describing his work towards the Commonwealth River Murray Act of 1915, which was supposed to have settled differences between New South Wales, Victoria, and South Australia over the use of inland rivers. But the disputes over the Murray-Darling waters have not disappeared, and now include the State of Queensland. Well over 60 per cent of Australian cotton, all grown in Queensland and New South Wales, depends on irrigation, has created ecological disasters, and deprives Victoria and South Australia of water that would otherwise be available. Glynn's arguments for the rights of all the involved States over interstate rivers and river systems remain as relevant as ever.

Furthermore, the principles that Glynn followed have not lost their significance in a world where climate change has become the defining challenge of our time. Drought, floods, and hurricanes have been triggering humanitarian crises across the globe. Likewise, his principles apply to debates on economic internationalism, as the world continues to cope with the impact of globalisation, as well as facing Brexit and the protectionist policies of the new American president.

Australia continues to have a high proportion of people born outside the country. Many migrants could draw inspiration from the struggles that Glynn faced after he arrived from Ireland and before his country of adoption let him win a place in the sun. He was helped to climb out of desperate poverty by the classical education he had received at high school and at Trinity College

Dublin. At a time in Australia when the study of Shakespeare and of Greek and Latin literature has gone into a severe decline, Glynn shows how such an education shapes a person for coping well with life. It also provided the platform for the courtesy, dedication to the common good, debating skills, and serious research that characterized Glynn's contribution as a federalist and politician. Does he serve as a role model at a time when the public has become more and more disillusioned by those who represent them in parliament? Australians need to know where we came from as a nation. They need to bring back to life the ideals which inspired Glynn and other founders of the Commonwealth of Australia. It is at our peril that we let those ideals fade from our national consciousness and life.

In my 1965 biography of Glynn, I described the struggle with which he maintained his Catholic faith. By the end of the nineteenth century, the challenge of agnostic scientists and philosophers had degraded the Christianity of many into little more than a vague deism, an acceptance of Christ as a moral guide, and a spirit of goodwill towards other human beings. In the face of new studies in comparative religion, it did not appear possible to defend the exclusive claims of Christian doctrine. Historical criticism seemed to have reduced the Bible to a merely human document from ancient times. Through all his intellectual religious difficulties, Glynn never wavered in the practice of his faith and commitment to improving the lives of others and serving the interests of the whole nation.

More than a century has passed since the Australian Commonwealth came into existence. Where Christianity once had a dominant voice, we have witnessed a radical secularization of social and political structures. At the time of Federation, just about everyone who married did so before a minister of religion. By 1999, over half of marriages were being performed by civil celebrants; by 2017, over three-quarters of those who decided to marry did so before civil celebrants. The legal definition of civil marriage now includes same-sex couples. Social institutions have changed strikingly since the days of Patrick McMahon Glynn, and illustrate dramatically the absence of God from public life. Do we need to hear once again the voice of a political leader who put an acknowledgement of God into our Constitution?

With all my family, I wish the PM Glynn Institute a flourishing future, which will continue to retrieve the ideals and example of my grandfather. More than ever, Australia needs to question an over-emphasis on the rights of autonomous individuals, respect the claims of common responsibilities, and honour duties that promote public wellbeing.

Anne Henderson has provided a brilliant overview of my grandfather's life and achievements. She repeatedly indicates how relevant his views remain on such issues as big government, free trade, land rights, the use of water resources, migrants, the delicate balance between religion, law, and the state, and the need for well informed and rational debate on these and other issues.

My thanks go out to the other contributors to this volume: Peter Boyce, John Fahey, Damien Freeman, Patrick Mullins, Suzanne Rutland, and Anne Twomey. From different angles, they have helped to re-introduce my grandfather to the Australian public just one hundred years since he left our national parliament.

Boyce's reflections on Anglicans made me think back over my thirty-three years on the staff of the Gregorian University in Rome. I enjoyed constant contacts with the Anglican Centre and its staff, housed in the Doria Palace right in the heart of the old city. This relationship shaped a growing friendship with the Archbishop of Canterbury, George Carey, and his wife Eileen. George wrote a foreword for three of my books, *Experiencing Jesus* (1994), *Following the Way* (1999), and *On the Left Bank of the Tiber* (2012). He also wrote a foreword for *The Convergence of Theology* (2001), a festschrift prepared in my honour by Daniel Kendall and Stephen T. Davis. My grandfather would have approved of all that ecumenism of the heart.

Gerald O'Collins SJ AC
Easter 2019
Jesuit Theological College, Parkville

Introduction

Damien Freeman

At the general elections in 1919, the Honourable Patrick McMahon Glynn KC MP lost his seat in the Commonwealth Parliament. He had entered the House of Representatives almost two decades earlier in 1901. He was the last of the Founding Fathers to sit in parliament.

In 2019, we mark the centenary of this milestone in Australia's political history, when the Founding Fathers handed over to the next generation. As a centrepiece of this commemoration, the PM Glynn Institute held the Gerald Glynn O'Collins Oration. This occasional lecture was named for Father O'Collins in recognition not only of his immense contribution to scholarship, but particularly in recognition of his work as author of the standard biography of his maternal grandfather, *Patrick McMahon Glynn: a founder of Australian federation* (1965) and editor of *Patrick McMahon Glynn: letters to his family (1874-1927)* (1974).

The Reverend Gerald Glynn O'Collins was born at Melbourne in 1931, and was educated at the University of Melbourne (MA 1st Hons 1959) and the University of Cambridge (PhD 1968), where he was also a research fellow of Pembroke College. He is a Jesuit priest, scholar, educator, and author or co-author of seventy-four books, including sixteen published by Oxford University Press. For more than three decades he was professor of systematic and fundamental theology at the Pontifical Gregorian University in Rome, where he was also dean of the theological faculty (1985-91). Currently he is a research fellow of the University of Divinity (Melbourne), adjunct professor of Australian Catholic University, and writer in residence at the Jesuit Theological College, Parkville. In 2006, he was created a Companion of the Order of Australia in recognition of his services to theology and ecumenism.

The oration was delivered by Anne Henderson, the deputy director of the Sydney Institute and a visiting fellow at the PM Glynn Institute. Her extensive publication list demonstrates her pursuit of knowledge about political history as well as the Catholic tradition in Australia and her career as a teacher in Catholic secondary schools demonstrates her commitment to education within the Catholic intellectual tradition and acting in truth and love. In 2015, she was appointed a Member of the Order of Australia for services to literature in the field of political history, and to the community by fostering public debate and discussion. In the same year, her book, *Menzies at War*, was shortlisted for the Prime Minister's Literary Award. Other publications include *From All Corners: Six Migrant Stories* (1993), *Educating Johannah: A Year in Year 12* (1995), *Mary McKillop's Sisters: A Life Unveiled* (1997), *Getting Even: Women MPs on Life Power and Politics* (1999), *Partners* (edited with R. Fitzgerald, 1999), *The Killing of Sister McCormack* (2002), *An Angel in the Court: The Life of Major Joyce Harmer* (2005), *Enid Lyons: Leading Lady to a Nation* (2008), and *Joseph Lyons: The People's Prime Minister* (2011), as well as contributions to *Australian Prime Ministers* (ed. M Grattan, 2000) and the *Dictionary of National Biography*.

The subject of Henderson's oration is the legacy of Father O'Collins's maternal grandfather, Patrick McMahon Glynn.

Glynn was born in Ireland, whence he emigrated to the colony of Victoria in 1880. His early years in Australia were difficult, but he eventually managed to establish himself in South Australia. He contributed significantly as a colonial politician, as a draftsman of the Australian Constitution, as a federal politician, as a Minister of the Crown, and as King's Counsel. He also took an active interest in matters relating to the Catholic Church in Australia, and remained committed to the affairs of his native Ireland. By any standard, his life was one of service and distinction – albeit service and distinction that might be forgotten with the passing of the years.

In 2017, the vice-chancellor, Greg Craven, established a public policy think-tank at Australian Catholic University, and chose to name it for Glynn. In so naming it, Craven might have intended that Glynn's life and achievements would provide inspiration for the think-tank's activities, and serve as an identifier for those in the wider community who would understand its aspirations through the association with its namesake. Perhaps, he had in mind the various other institutes, research centres, foundations, and societies that have been named after the likes of John Curtin, Ben Chifley, H. V. Evatt, E. G. Whitlam, R. G. Menzies, and Sir Samuel Griffith. It will, no doubt, be immediately apparent to most readers that, however worthy Glynn may be of a place in such a pantheon of former Australian statesmen and jurists, there would be very few circles in which his name would be as instantly recognisable as theirs are today. Whilst the current volume does not pretend to ensure Glynn's brand recognition, it is published in the hope that it will go some way towards reintroducing his name and legacy to a new generation.

The PM Glynn Institute was honoured to have Anne

Henderson as a visiting fellow in 2019. At the core of this volume is an essay that is the fruit of the researches that she undertook when preparing to deliver the Gerald Glynn O'Collins Oration on Glynn's legacy for a nation.

Henderson has not sought to provide a standard biography of Glynn as O'Collins did in 1965. Her essay is intended to introduce Glynn to a new generation, so that those who are interested might seek out the O'Collins biography, in which they will find a comprehensive account of Glynn's life. Henderson's essay provides a sketch of Glynn's life before emigrating from Ireland to Australia; the story of how he came to Kapunda in South Australia, and found prosperity there; his marriage to Abigail Dynon; and his career as a colonial and federal politician. She also offers us an assessment of some of the key contributions that he made to public life through the debate about land nationalisation in South Australia; his place in the federation movement and the drafting of the Australian Constitution; his involvement with managing the Murray-Darling river system; his attitude to Home Rule for Ireland and the British throne; and his attempts to prevent the deportation of Father Charles Jerger when the hysteria surrounding British subjects of German ancestry in Australia was at its peak during and after World War I. Finally, Henderson concludes by providing an assessment of what she regards as Glynn's enduring legacy for the nation that he helped to found. It is notable that she draws attention not only to his achievements, but also to his personal qualities – many of which she finds lacking in public life today. The implication is that today's politicians would do well to reflect on Glynn's conduct in public life, and to temper their own conduct accordingly.

This publication marks a departure from the usual activities of the PM Glynn Institute, which is ordinarily concerned with contributing to discussions about public philosophy and public policy. In 2018, it partnered with Uphold & Recognise to establish a policy unit that produced *Upholding the Big Ideas*, a set of options papers for constitutional recognition of Aboriginal and Torres Strait Islander peoples. In the same year, it established the Kapunda Press, which published two books – *Chalice of Liberty: Protecting religious freedom in Australia* and *Today's Tyrants: Responding to Dyson Heydon* – a collection of essays about J. D. Heydon's inaugural PM Glynn Lecture on Religion, Law and Public Life. This will be followed by *The Market's Morals: Responding to Jesse Norman*, which discusses the second lecture, delivered by Jesse Norman MP in 2018. In 2019, the Kapunda Press will also publish a collection entitled *Nonsense on Stilts: Rescuing human rights in Australia* and Adrian Pabst's *Story of Our Country: The ALP's ethical purpose from Curtin to Shorten*. The Institute has also produced a pamphlet entitled *Amen: A history of prayers in Parliament*, which provides some context for discussions about whether the Victorian Parliament should discontinue its current practice of reciting daily prayers. It is to be hoped that the present volume's reflections on the PM Glynn Institute's namesake will serve as a reminder of the spirit in which he would approach these other activities.

Henderson's essay is presented with five short responses. Patrick Mullins discusses Henderson's approach to Glynn's life, and some of the more profound themes that her treatment reveals. Anne Twomey extends Henderson's discussion by reflecting further on the impact of Glynn's religion on his public life, and his approach to the law, particularly as Attorney-General. Glynn's

Catholic experience is then compared with the experience of his Jewish contemporary, Sir Isaac Isaacs, by Suzanne Rutland, and placed in the context of Anglican prejudices by Peter Boyce. Finally, John Fahey compares Henderson's account of a Catholic in public life with his own experience more than half a century later.

In their different ways, each of the essays in this volume reminds us of some aspect of Patrick McMahon Glynn's legacy – as an independent thinker, a prolific writer, a popular speaker, a passionate advocate for issues that he thought were important for Australia, and so much more. On 5 October 1904, Glynn said in the House of Representatives:

> Considering the record of mistakes that legislators have made, we ought to keep the State to its true province, which is to destroy monopoly, to afford to all equal opportunity, and to leave to private enterprise, to individual intelligence and guidance, the task of perfecting and sustaining what is best in our industrial and social civilisation.

In Glynn's day, the parliament met in Melbourne. He was voted out long before the first Parliament House was built in Canberra, and the politicians moved into the Canberra bubble. A century later, Glynn remains an outstanding example of leadership in public life, of the Catholic contribution to Federation, and of how conviction and service can be brought together in politics. Perhaps, he even holds the key to bursting the Canberra bubble.

Chronology

1855	25 August	Patrick McMahon Glynn born in Gort, Ireland
1880	4 September	embarks for Australia on The Orient
	16 October	arrives and settles in Melbourne
1882	2 July	arrives in Adelaide to start work with law firm of Hardy and Davis; in August, he opens a new branch of the firm at the mining town of Kapunda, north of Adelaide
1883	April	accepted the editorship of the Kapunda Herald which he would edit until 1891 alongside his work as a lawyer
1886		buys the Kapunda legal practice
1884		helps found the South Australian Land Nationalisation Society and writes its manifesto
1887		elected as junior member for the seat of Light in South Australia
1888		moves to live in Adelaide and open a practice there, but keeps his practice at Kapunda
1890		loses his seat at the election
1895		wins a seat for North Adelaide in a by-election
1896		loses his seat at election
1897		wins his seat of North Adelaide again in a by-election
		elected also as one of ten delegates to the Australasian Federation Conventions
	11 September	married Abigail Dynon in Melbourne
1898		third and final convention in Melbourne where, on 2 March, Glynn moved successfully the motion that the words "humbly relying on the blessing of Almighty God" be inserted in the preamble to the Commonwealth of Australia Constitution Act
1901		elected as a Free Trader to the inaugural parliament of Australia in a state-wide election (South Australia did not make use of electorates in this election)
1903		returned for the federal seat of Angus
1905		prepared two volumes of legal opinion on the Murray riparian rights for the South Australian government
1909-10		Attorney-General in the Deakin (Fusion) government
1913-14		Minister for External Affairs in the Cook (Liberal) government
1916		visited United Kingdom and France as part of an Empire delegation to inspect the war administration
1917-19		Minister for Home and Territories in the Hughes government
1919		lost his seat at the election but continued to work for some years as a barrister
1931	28 October	died at home in North Adelaide

The Gerald Glynn O'Collins Oration

Federation's man of letters

Anne Henderson

He died at the height of the Great Depression on 28 October 1931 at his home in North Adelaide. As the most significant Catholic figure to have risen on the non-Labor side of Australian politics, in his last months Glynn may have also noted that another non-Labor Catholic of Irish background – Joseph Lyons – was by then close to taking the keys to the Lodge in Canberra. In his declining years, Patrick McMahon Glynn KC, one of the founding fathers of the Australian federation, former colonial and federal MP, and minister in the Deakin, Cook and Hughes governments, might well have also reflected how the boom-and-bust economy of the Land Down Under had come full circle as his star rose over half a century.

Yet much had moved on. In his native Ireland, for which he had long ago advocated Home Rule in a union with Britain, an Irish Free State, albeit bitterly and bloodily won, now governed the southern twenty-six counties separated from the six counties of Northern Ireland. In Canberra, the fledgling federal Commonwealth Paddy Glynn had helped fashion, in extraordinary last-minute moves as the nineteenth century folded, had finally begun to emerge as a physical presence with a scattering of buildings among paddocks of grazing sheep. The new Parliament House (now Old Parliament House) stood isolated and proud, fronting newly planted avenues and occasional newly constructed buildings housing select departments.

Glynn's foresight and argument for a single-gauge railway track across the former colonies had not succeeded but, with the aid of timetable connections at the borders, MPs and visitors could now travel to Canberra by rail via Sydney and Melbourne. Radio and telecommunication were fast overtaking the postal services Glynn had relied on so often in his heavy collection of letters left to his family now housed in the National Library in Canberra. The River Murray Waters Agreement of 1915, in which Glynn played a key role, had taken shape, its locks and storage facilities ensuring navigation of the river for trade in South Australia from Wentworth at the Murray-Darling junction to farmers and others downstream. Glynn would have been stunned to think that his advocacy for South Australia's water rights would have echoes a century later.

In the debate over protection and free trade, Glynn had sided with George Reid's Free Traders and so marked himself out amongst the conservative side of politics. The case for free trade would not be won for many decades after Glynn's death, yet free trade between the States had succeeded in the coming together of the colonies at federation. For all that, in his early years as a colonial MP (1887-1890), he also supported payment for members of parliament, female suffrage, and reform of the upper house, which aligned him with the more liberal side of politics. In his 1899 campaign for the South Australian seat of North Adelaide, one of his strongest supporters and campaigners was the leading suffragist Catherine Spence.[1] In his years as a federal MP, Glynn was often praised for the advice he gave MPs on all sides of the debates.

As federal parliament, on 29 October 1931, eulogised the passing of one of its founding MPs, Labor prime minister Jim

Scullin remarked of Glynn, "Every honourable member who had the privilege of knowing him intimately was proud to claim him as a friend. He will be remembered as a great scholar, and a cultured and eloquent speaker on occasions of importance. . . . To members of all parties he was always ready to give valuable advice and assistance." Senator George Pearce, speaking of his one-time colleague, affirmed that Glynn "was an enthusiastic Australian, a loyal British subject, a man of wide reading, and a great Shakespearean scholar. The flashes that came from his fertile mind illumed many a debate, and apt quotations from the philosophers of old gave a charm and grace to many of his speeches."

Sir Robert Menzies, commenting on Glynn, whom he would have come to know years earlier as a barrister appearing before the High Court sitting in Melbourne, described him as "looking like a black beetle and talking like a silver-tongued angel".[2]

Standing not so tall at 165 centimetres, Glynn often was regarded as having the build of a jockey. His love of horses and notable membership of the Adelaide Hunt Club added to his jockey character. His grandson, Gerald O'Collins SJ, in his memoir of Glynn, describes him as "a popular figure and a bold huntsman, although never a stylish rider . . . but he made up for any defects of technique by his capacity for hard knocks and broken ribs, arms and collar-bones."[3] Sir Robert Garran, recalling federation personalities, wrote, "He was a reckless rider to hounds, and must have broken more bones in the hunting-field than any other man in Australia."[4] As his reputation grew, satirists and cartoonists pictured Glynn more and more with an oversized head and willowy frame, topped off with his characteristic bushy moustache.

The Patrick McMahon Glynn story reflects much about the age he belonged to and the wider British society he both came from and would move through, in time and location. But his ideas, independently argued over decades, often forecast debates to come. Who could have imagined that colonial debate over States' rights at the federation conventions in 1897 and 1898, over Glynn's motion to have a recognition of God in the preamble to the Commonwealth of Australia Constitution Act, would ripple down the decades more than a century later with a federal government *Religious Freedom Review* that recommended in part a wholesale overriding of State jurisdictions in order to protect the rights of religious believers following changes to the Marriage Act in 2017?

Maev O'Collins, Glynn's granddaughter, reminded readers of *The Age* on 8 April 1992 that, "On 18 February 1898, Patrick McMahon Glynn, one of the South Australian delegates to the Federal Convention, wrote in the Sydney newspaper *Australian Star* that, 'We cannot shut our eyes to the fact that the theatre of the world's struggle is being shifted from West to East . . . the time may come when England will tell us that she has other duties to which she must subordinate the defence of Australia, and ask her [Australia] to herself secure her standing in the counsels of Eastern Asia.'"[5]

The immigrant

Patrick McMahon Glynn made his way to Australia from Ireland in 1880, leaving from Plymouth on 4 September. He was twenty-five. An articled clerk in Dublin, a graduate of Trinity College Dublin, and a student of the law at Middle Temple in London, Glynn was trying his luck in the Australian colonies where he hoped to prosper, as he had not done at the bar in Ireland where he had returned from London to begin his legal career.

Leaving England's shores, Glynn wrote in his diary of his poor prospects in Dublin where he had hoped to make a living only to encounter an empty brief bag: ". . . the ills of the flesh are sometimes experienced in the stomach, and the prospect of ultimate but remote success compensated little for the pressure of adversity in the few sunny days of life. In Ireland, energy and ability are only one of the prerequisites for professional success . . . I shake hands with the past and take my hat off to the future."[6]

Glynn's connections to the colonies Down Under included several members of the Glynn and Wallsh families, among whom was his mother's sister, Mother Bernard Wallsh, subsequently Mother General of Mary MacKillop's Josephite order. It was an age where religion defined one's place in British society in multiple ways, with the sectarian divisions of Christianity separating Catholic and Protestant into clubby support groups, while notions abounded that religious observance bred good moral character and the unbelieving could well be equated with the great unwashed. On board Glynn's steamship *Orient* he recorded a few days out from Plymouth that, "Temperance and Bible meetings [have] given origin to some opposition in the steerage".

Glynn, like many an Irishman of his day, walked two worlds – Catholic and Protestant. The Catholic one had nurtured and guided him from childhood, albeit a middle-class one from the hard-earned success of his family of west-coast merchants in the town of Gort. Surviving amid the destitution of many, this upbringing had instilled in Glynn a collective memory of prejudice, repression and struggle – as he would go on to opine in a parliamentary debate on 17

August 1905, commenting on the impoverishment of the Irish under the yoke of Britain, "[While] some of us have never known what it is to feel want, have never been deprived of a meal, and have never had a moment's anxiety as to the possibilities of the future, we may perhaps understand the occasional fierceness that is characteristic of Irish agitation."[7] In his 30,000 word *Manifesto* for the South Australian Land Nationalisation Society in 1884, Glynn recorded Ireland's over-production of wheat from lands owned by absentee landlords during Ireland's famine, where on "roads by which thousands lay down to die of starvation was heard the rattle of the wheat carts on their way to the ports of exportation."[8] From his Catholic background, Glynn also inherited perseverance and the courage of tribal loyalty.

But the Protestant world of British political and literary traditions would give Glynn his intellectual ambition, a path to success and many of the principles and heroes he lived by – Milton, Shakespeare, Burke, Carlyle, Mill, De Quincey, Chatham, and so on. His hero for political style and thought was undoubtedly Edmund Burke, an eighteenth-century Whig whose writings and political record still inspire. In an article for the *Austral Light* in February 1913, Glynn wrote: "In the days of simpler, if more inspiring, themes, speakers had not to analyse and marshal the multifarious details of modern affairs. Burke could present a mass of matter and method and clearness while attaining, as occasion required, an ancient finish. . . . Burke was above the House of Commons, and never appeared like himself, but when forgetful of idle clamours of party, and of the little views of little men, he appealed to his country, and the enlightened judgement of mankind."[9] When Glynn delivered a speech on Burke in November 1897, *The Advertiser* reported that he had praised Burke as an MP for Bristol for refusing "to sacrifice his mature opinions and judgment on the questions of Catholic relief and Irish trade laws to the prejudice of the constituents".[10]

Glynn's Catholic faith would hold him near and guide his personal choices, but it would also challenge him. From early adulthood, more and more, his values would be formed independently with the depth and breadth of his reading and his personal growth in the cheek-by-jowl buffering of colonial settlement in Australia. In a world where the institutional church wielded enormous influence, Glynn, like others from time to time, questioned the worldly and material perspectives of some church leaders. Writing to his brother James on 21 March 1886, he commented on the passing of the Anglican Bishop of Manchester, a Dr Fraser: "We are sending you home Bishop Moorhouse, late of Melbourne, a man of wide and scholarly culture and great liberality to fill the see of Manchester. . . . His predecessor, Dr Fraser, died leaving £85,000 at his bankers, not a bad sum to get for dinning into his flock's ears that it is 'more difficult for a rich man to get to Heaven etc'. This is not what the example of Jesus taught those who call themselves his disciples."[11]

Not only the well-heeled Anglicans gave Glynn pause over the way church finances often clashed with more spiritual matters in the ways of institutional religion. Early in his time at his first legal practice in South Australia's Kapunda, Glynn was startled at the amount of money local organisations extracted from locals by way of subscriptions. But, as he told his mother in a letter home on 26 September 1882, nothing quite matched the wholesale robbery of the local Catholic priest: "When I tell you that last Sunday at Mass a subscription for the Catholic Refuge took place at the Last Gospel and that the priest actually afterwards ensured all the male congregation into staying in Church after Mass on plea of a matter of importance, then locked the doors, and would let no fellow out under half a guinea, you will all smile, and perhaps even laugh, incredulously. *But it's a fact*. He ran into debt over some graveyard and of course stuck up all the heavily mulcted farmers. I came back to my hotel a sadder, a wiser, and, by 13/- [shillings], a lighter man."[12]

Assessing the men of the federation assemblies, the Protestant Alfred Deakin wrote that Glynn was "the best read man of the Convention, [and] certainly carried more English prose and poetry in his memory than any three or four of his associates".[13] Another Protestant colleague, Sir Robert Garran, concurred, writing that Glynn had "a prodigious memory . . . [and] was a fine speaker [who] showed signs of careful preparation."[14]

Docking in Melbourne on 16 October 1880, after a brief stop at Adelaide, Glynn was far from the distinguished Australian he would become. Like all migrants there was the inevitable shock of the new. He could have been seen walking Melbourne's dusty environs ("Oculists and public houses succeed well here. The amount of dust capable of being inhaled may have something to do with their prosperity")[15] looking very much the New Chum in the crowd, taking in the reality of his new situation as opposed to the imagined world of his hopes. "The City, as I said, is not *built* yet," he wrote to his mother on 11 November 1880, "A timber shanty is next door neighbour to a princely bank."[16]

For a well-educated Irishman like Glynn, Melbourne's brash egalitarian rawness took him by surprise. Towards the end of 1880, reviewing his impressions of his new city in his diary,

Glynn reflected, "Class distinctions exist in Melbourne in a greater degree than at home. . . . But the existence of caste here has more disagreeable concomitants than elsewhere, the levelling up tendency of the lower classes is the result of the assumption of an independence of manner, made up of the absence of all courtesy and politeness; while among the upper ten vulgarity and wealth are very often associated. Aristocracy is not indicative of refinement, nor plebeian of mannerly deference."[17]

For all his ruminations on the negatives, Glynn appreciated that Marvellous Melbourne was a city, for its age, that was going places – even if he was not going far at that point. His letter of introduction to the Supreme Court's Redmond Barry, a graduate of Trinity College Dublin, who around that time was presiding over Ned Kelly's trial, earned him lunch and a few curt words of advice that Glynn should not waste his time in the Australian colonies as a 'migrant' lawyer and go back to Dublin. Sir John O'Shannassy, thrice premier of Victoria and a Catholic, gave him more encouragement that he could get started, but was of little assistance.[18]

For all his learning and professional background, Glynn would find his early experience as an immigrant as challenging as any unskilled equivalent, even as the economy supposedly boomed ahead of the 1890s depression. The legal world in Melbourne worked as a collection of cronies, shutting out newcomers. With romantic optimism and in an attempt to publicise his name, Glynn invested in producing two thousand copies of a pamphlet entitled *Irish State Trials*. The black comedy of this failed investment is well documented in Gerald O'Collins's memoir of his grandfather, alongside Glynn's unsuccessful attempts to use whatever connection he could advance in his favour – his good name and background getting him introductions to leaders such as the premier of Victoria and the mayor of Melbourne.

Over the next year and more, the penury of boarding-house existence, an assortment of Irish relatives of little note and with dysfunctional personal lives, and the saving grace, on occasion, of the pawnshop not only tested his endurance but gave Patrick McMahon Glynn a taste of the underclass, an experience he would recall in later years when showing empathy for those less fortunate. In spite of his conservatism and rejection of radical or intemperate moves, Glynn had something of the Irish tendency to tilt at privileged elites who presided over injustice. In this, Glynn revered Burke's involvement in the trial of Warren Hastings and condemnation of Hastings's actions in India. On the other hand, and with a similar tendency to kick up, Glynn did not go along with his hero Edmund Burke's support for the French monarchy in the uproar and bloodshed of the French Revolution. As he wrote to his brother Joseph on 6 March 1892, "What Burke did for the principle of ordered growth was invaluable, but had I been alive in those days and in France I would have stood by Danton and his crew, when we read of Marie Antoinette and her rakish frivolities."

Near bankruptcy at times in these early Melbourne days, Glynn did not give up on his ambition of making his way intellectually and in public life. Alongside his futile efforts of appearing daily around the courts in the hope of advancement, Glynn's comfort was a set time for reading before the end of each day. Of Christmas Day 1881, he recorded, "I spent the day in the Botanical Gardens reading my constant companion Shakespeare."[19]

As any hope faded that an opening for a legal career might

eventuate, Glynn wrote home saying he needed to try standing for parliament. He had joined the Fitzroy branch of the Conservative Reform Association and was a founding member of Melbourne's Irish Land League. He was making speeches to large audiences. "My name gets known as my pocket gets empty," he wrote in his diary on 22 June 1881. When what he referred to in his diary as the job of "canvasser for lives* and Singer Sewing machines", came his way in January 1882, he set off for country Victoria. The situation offered bare food and lodging but his ironic accounts of those weeks on the road, with his lack of commercial success and the bush characters he met along the way, make entertaining reading. In a recognisable Irish style, Glynn kept smiling through his troubles, with an old-fashioned perseverance and, in spite of genuine misery in many of his diary scribblings, an inexplicable optimism that something would turn up. A rare cheque from home kept him from complete bankruptcy.

A change in Glynn's personal outlook was slowly evolving. In spite of his reservations about a society with rough manners and overly protected upper echelons, Glynn had found a freedom he could never have imagined back home. It was the freedom of many an immigrant; the freedom that had developed new worlds far from old Europe over successive generations. In part, Glynn's diary reads like the jottings of a sojourner-adventurer, sucking in the new experiences of an explorer traveller:

> Living in that haphazard fashion, getting a meal wherever
> hospitality offered one and fasting in other cases, is not a
> course of life I would recommend many people. . . . The

---

* Glynn was canvassing for the Mutual Life Assurance Society ("lives") and the sewing machine company simultaneously.

Iron mines at Lal Lal are situated on the summit of one of several hills separated by deep gorges, and command a lovely view of Egerton in the distance. The means of access to them is dangerous except with a trusty horse and driver, being over a narrow cutting, which winds along the sides of the hills. But I would risk my life once more in driving over it again in the dark to witness such another spectacle as was presented by the blood-red glare of a bush fire towards Geelong on the second night of our visit.[20]

Still, with penury stalking him – a "four months state of starvation and poverty" as Glynn recorded of late 1881 – he had been ready to accept a job taking him to New Zealand.[21] One was proposed but never eventuated. He had also considered moving to Sydney, although lack of funds made the fare and resettlement a risk. In all of this, he never thought of going back to Britain, not even Ireland. Then, an opening arrived – thanks to his aunt, Mother Bernard Wallsh of the Sisters of St Joseph. A representative of a firm of solicitors in Adelaide had been in contact with her. They were looking for what Glynn referred to as "a Roman Catholic Irishman" to open a legal practice in the country district of Kapunda just north of Adelaide. For once the Catholic club had smiled on him. Glynn took the job.

Kapunda

Writing to his mother on 5 July 1882, Glynn assured her that, while he had made a fortunate move, it was not one he hoped to make permanent:

> I am by no means inclined to settle here. In fact I felt more down hearted at this change than ever in my life. I suppose it was the result of having been exposed [to] the pelting of many a pitiless storm in Victoria that made me lonely

when I left it. But I must pay my debts, put some clothes
on my back and some money in my pocket. When I have
a couple of hundred pounds saved I can change again. . . .
Your affectionate son, P. McM Glynn[22]

What followed was no easy path. Until he bought the
Kapunda practice outright in 1886, Glynn preferred to remain
on his three pounds a week salary as a 'clerk' to the partners
Hardy and Davis.[23] Kapunda in the 1880s, a town of some 3,000,
was suffering a downturn in its mining operations and a drought
for farmers. In his early years, Glynn's days were taken up in
much travel for clients who contributed lean pickings. He would
not have persisted at the practice had he not been offered, and
had taken, the editorship of the *Kapunda Herald* in April 1883.
The payments for his work as editor were regular and gratefully
received.

As such, Glynn's name and significance became recognised
more widely. On St Patrick's Day in 1883, he noted in his diary
that he had been one of the prominent locals invited to sit on the
platform, before giving the vote of thanks, as the parish priest,
Father Williams, read a lecture on St Patrick in the Institute
Hall.[24] By September that year, Glynn was significant beyond his
local Catholic community when the Adelaide *Register* (later the
Advertiser) reproduced his leader on parliamentary privileges –
a first for the *Kapunda Herald*. He was called on to propose the
health of parliament at the Kapunda and the Light Agricultural
Society's Show. Unlikely as it could have been imagined, Glynn
would begin his political climb in a mining town, 80 kilometres
north of Adelaide.

Patrick McMahon Glynn carried no alienation in his
identity as a citizen of the British Empire. From his approach

to Home Rule for Ireland to his aspirations for the emerging Commonwealth of Australia, his support for the Crown was unambiguous, all of which in time endeared him to a majority of his political colleagues. His position on solutions for Irish Home Rule backed Ireland being part of the United Kingdom, as part of a federation. He condemned Sir Roger Casement for his role in the Easter Rising in 1916.

Yet, to a great extent, Glynn's experience as an Irishman governed a lot of his leanings. He was an admirer of Henry George and his ideas on land tax to break up monopolies of land ownership. As Glynn put it in the House of Representatives in 1910, "I do not know why some states have for so long allowed their water frontages to be monopolised by particular persons. One born in the old country has still a sort of reflex antipathy to certain ownerships in Australia, as a result of the experiences of one's childhood, when a man dared not cross from one field to another, or take the slightest advantage of those opportunities of peaceful enjoyment given by rivers." Many Indigenous Australians might have read Glynn's views on Australia's land monopolies and sympathised.

In Glynn's editorials for the *Kapunda Herald*, over the best part of a decade, is to be found the evolution of a very independent political stance. While Kapunda was home to a significant number of Irish who had migrated to the colony and worked in the mining town, it was still unusual to have a local paper which, from time to time, editorialised on Home Rule and the question of Ireland. On Friday, 23 September 1887, the *Kapunda Herald* opined, "John Stuart Mill called the Conservative Party the stupid party. If Mill were alive today he would not feel inclined to withdraw the epithet. . . . What is certain is that the Conservatives and their accidental supporters are not going to put down free speech in Ireland . . . the rejection of Mr Parnell's Rent Bill has led to nothing but disaster. . . . The cry of Home Rule cannot be met by describing the anticipated results as utopian."

Glynn's wide reading, especially of much overseas press delivered to him by post, seasoned the same editorials with an enrichment of global thinking, and a multitude of ambitious advocacy. On 9 September 1887, the *Kapunda Herald* took up the vexed issue of tariffs and protection, arguing that tariffs at ten and fifteen per cent were raising prices up to thirty and forty per cent. "This is not mere conjecture," argued the editor, "We see it exemplified in the United States and in Victoria. The highly protected Victorian industries want more protection, and many of them would collapse at once were the duties reduced by even one third. . . . The new tariff is not intended to start industries. It is simply to raise prices and the customer will have to pay the piper. It will not lead to a dozen men being employed who could not have found work without it. The working men will get no share of the spoils."

Glynn's views on protection would not change over time. In the move to federate the colonies, Glynn saw free trade as an imperative: "Though the protectionist element only may be represented by the Assembly's delegates," he wrote on 22 July 1890, after the Australasian Federation Conference in February, "they have nearly all been forced to recognise that federation without inter-colonial free trade would be an anomaly."[25]

It was indeed a mix of liberalism and conservatism that drove Glynn. As the heated debates on alien migration to the colonies intensified, Glynn was with the majority in thinking that competition from cheap Pacific (Kanaka) and Asian (Chinese) labour would only degrade the wages of the colonies' European working men – just as some twenty million Hispanic illegal immigrants in the United States have kept wages and conditions well below Australian standards over decades.[26] Yet, in his editorials, Glynn was also able to give voice to consideration of the rights of Chinese wanting to settle in the colonies.

On 18 May 1888, Glynn editorialised against New South Wales premier Henry Parkes after his drastic measures to limit New South Wales's intake of Chinese immigrants: "Sir Henry Parkes forgets that his colony is a part of the British Empire. . . . It is of far more consequence that the honour of England should be maintained than that a few hundred Chinamen, coming here under existing treaties, should be prevented from landing." And, again, on 1 June 1888, "A curious commentary upon the allegation that the Chinese bid fair to swamp us, is the fact that in 1881 the number of Chinese in all the colonies was only 1,706 more than the 42,000 in Victoria alone in 1859. Between 1859 and 1881 the Chinese in Victoria diminished in number from 42,000 to 12,000, while from 1881 to 1886 they only increased 130." It was also, in Glynn's measured logic, an attempt to take the hysteria out of the debate.

After a year in South Australia, Glynn was writing to his mother that while the large income he had been promised had not been forthcoming, still he was managing financially and at last was to be admitted to the South Australian bar. Kapunda, the "Liliputian" city as he called it, was the victim of troubled times for its mining and farming businesses but she must not think it a "very bad place". He went on, "We have a big public dance once a fortnight – a lawn tennis club, private parties etc. and a general air of smartness in everything compared to a provincial town at home. However, these are things I reckon very little. As long as I think that I might have beaten a few fools in a bigger sphere of action, I can never remain quiet."[27]

Certainly, Glynn was not one to spend long hours socialising. He made a firm friend of a Kapunda doctor named Hamilton, a graduate of Trinity College Dublin, and on hot and windy nights they reminisced about the old country and its wild Atlantic shores. At Institute dances, one anonymous Kapunda resident recalled him as beginning "diffidently" and then "gaining confidence".[28] For all that, as he wrote to his mother, "With the exception of the dances, the people have kindly consented to leave me alone. In fact, reading Parliamentary debates, Bills, Politics Colonial and foreign, in addition to the office, permits of no leisure for gossip, especially when there are so many good books in the world unread."[29]

There were games of cards with local bachelors and boarding-house mates, race meetings where he lost as much as he ever won, the tennis club, and occasional visits to prominent family homes. He had spasmodic bouts of loneliness and mused at times that he was in want of a wife. He enjoyed the theatre and musical evenings and became a teetotaller off the back of a wager from a Shakespearean actress, Annie Mayor, in January 1883 that he and Mayor's brother give up alcohol for a month. Glynn never drank again.[30]

In his diary entry for 25 October 1884, Glynn notes his meeting with the pretty Maggie Disher of Woodside who was to spend a month in Kapunda. Her sudden appearance seems to have affected Glynn who, in the same entry, complained of the "abundance of devilish ugly women to be met in South Australia", as if Miss Disher reminded him of what he had been missing. Over some weeks, Miss Maggie appeared in brief mentions in the diary, playing doubles at the tennis club and so on, only to drop out of Glynn's Kapunda life on 21 November on the 10.20 am train. Wrote Glynn of his feelings: "Funny world this. I believe I would walk to Gawler and back tonight . . . just to meet her for a few minutes, and yet I never felt this so until she was gone."[31]

Miss Disher and Glynn crossed paths occasionally in the next few months, but the moment had passed. On 12 May 1885, Glynn recorded in his diary that he had bought a three-and-a-half-year-old filly for £17 which he was having broken in. As his professional star rose, Glynn was more likely to be found at the hunt club than the dance meeting.

Land nationalisation, the single tax and Teutons

In 1978, celebrated free-market economist Milton Friedman declared a tax on the unimproved value of land to be "the least bad tax". This was an echo of a past long forgotten. American economist Henry George, in the late nineteenth century, had popularised the idea of a tax on the unimproved value of land. Indeed, his writings had such ambition that George calculated such a tax could replace all other taxes – a veritable single tax to fund modern government. George's book *Progress and Poverty*, published in 1879, sold more copies in America in the 1890s than any other book except the Bible and spawned campaigns for land-value taxation around the world. In 2018, as younger citizens across the Western world became increasingly locked out of home ownership in modern cities like London and

Sydney, an article for *The Economist* discussed ideas around Henry George's land tax as worthy of consideration.[32]

In Kapunda, Glynn became enamoured with George's ideas. His early record of George in his diaries came on 14 February 1884, when he mentions William Webster, an associate of George. After giving a lecture in Kapunda, George was leaving South Australia: "On 9th January, Henry George began his series of lectures on the land question in England at London. Webster often told me about this campaign; some of George's letters to him make mention of it." On 28 March, he noted in his diary entry that he was reading George's *Social Problems*. In April 1884, after the South Australian elections at which Glynn had been urged to stand as a candidate but declined, the South Australian Land Nationalisation Society was founded to promote ideas such as those of George with Glynn one of three vice-presidents.

The South Australian Land Nationalisation Society's Manifesto was the beginning of Glynn's political career – not that he would have recognised it as such at the time. For all his leaders in the *Kapunda Herald* and memberships of the Irish Land League and the Fitzroy branch of the Conservative Reform Association in his first year in Melbourne, the work he was to do with the *Manifesto* and the ideas of Henry George marked him out as part of a political movement.

Writing to his brother James on 20 October 1884, Glynn revealed that he was the author of the South Australian Land Nationalisation Society's *Manifesto*. His diary entry of 15 July that year records his having finished the draft: "Have just finished the Manifesto of the South Australian Land Nationalisation Society. It covers 176 pages of leader manuscript. A load thereby removed." Glynn was giving lectures near and far on the ideas of Henry George and the land tax. He had, after four years in the colonies, begun to call Australia home. Writing to James, Glynn opined: "When we parted at Euston, neither of us probably thought much of what were to be the subsequent *facts*, so seldom do conjectures come right. You are now very likely as certain to remain at home as I am to remain here – not from real preference, but people never make allowance for the decadence of old and the birth of new associations."[33]

The *Manifesto* pulled no punches. Writing anonymously, Glynn gave vent to an inner sense of injustice rarely seen in his editorials. Ownership of land, the *Manifesto* asserted, had become one of the great thefts of people's rights. Nothing less than the abolition of private ownership of land could restore justice to ordinary citizens:

> About a million and a quarter acres of the best agricultural land in South Australia, situated within the line of rainfall, is at present owned by about thirty persons. It seems unjust on the face of it that population should be driven to settle upon the arid plains of the north, while such vast tracts of suitable country nearer home are not put to their proper uses.

The "proper uses" Glynn referred to was small farming for agricultural purposes not grazing. It was revolutionary stuff, however, to argue for a wholesale nationalisation of land for South Australia.

In his *Manifesto,* Glynn went back to Norman times, the era of King Henry VIII, and the land reforms of the seventeenth and eighteenth centuries that stripped tenant farmers of their subsistence plots. Thus, he demonstrated how the common good had so often been abused by the monopoly of land possession. Such capitalisation of land not only diminished the capital available from leases for the government, but also ended with ordinary citizens being held to ransom by a small number of landowners, in many cases absentees. For readers of the *Manifesto* a century and more on, it could be said that Glynn was making fundamental arguments for the government to retain control of its public ownership – in other words resist the privatisation of public utilities and assets, as well as Crown land.

The theme of closer settlement, or arguments for reducing the monopolies of pastoralists and property owners, would recur in Australia's history of land distribution over decades – echoed in the selection acts of the nineteenth century, closer settlement policies in Tasmania in the early 1900s that a youthful Labor MP, Joseph Lyons, would argue for, and the land settlement/closer settlement schemes of B. A. Santamaria's National Catholic Rural Movement of the 1940s and 1950s. Labor leader Bill Shorten's policies, in 2019, aiming to reform negative gearing of investment properties to make it easier for those without property to buy their own homes, have a similar motivation.

According to the *Manifesto*, as players in the system of representative government, the power to bring about reform and social equality lay with those who had the vote. In South Australia, for the House of Assembly, this was males over 21 who had lived at the same address for six months. As the *Manifesto* states: "The most superficial knowledge of history is enough to make it plain that no great popular revolution has ever come from above – the masses themselves have started and forced them all." Drawing on the experience of the dispossession of tenant farmers in Britain over centuries, Glynn made plain the suffering of generations. Closer to his own life experience were the absentee landlords of Ireland and land laws that threw tenant farmers off their land, sending thousands of his fellow Irish citizens onto ships heading for North America and Australia:

> The same tendency to convert arable into pasture land was at this period also becoming general in Ireland, and propagated itself throughout succeeding reigns; but, although the consequences were far more serious in that country where the refuge of industrial pursuits was not open to the evicted, the State allowed matters to proceed until agrarian outrages had arisen. Appalling misery was the result.[34]

In the *Manifesto*, Glynn drew parallels with South Australia where the land was plentiful but not a lot of it habitable. Here, too, ownership of large tracts of land remained in the hands of a few wealthy. But land should be universally owned:

> "When," says John Stuart Mill, "the sacredness of property is talked about, it should always be remembered that any such sacredness does not belong in the same degree to landed property. No man made land. It is the original inheritance of the whole species. Its appropriation is wholly a question of general expediency. When private property in land is not expedient it is unjust."[35]

The history of European settlement in Australia revolves around land and rights to land. Under the global order that has prevailed since 1788 on the continent known as Australia, Indigenous Australians have also come to understand what that means. Moreover, in the historic Mabo decision in the High Court in June 1992, the Commonwealth of Australia came to accept that Indigenous rights to land pre-dated that 1788 order, leading to numerous successful Indigenous claims to tracts of

Australia's territory. Land and its acquisition have long since been a means to prosperity in Australia. Even Glynn himself, aged 42, would become a property owner – initially of 44 Molesworth St, North Adelaide – after his marriage to Abigail Dynon. As he recorded in his diary for 8 June 1898, with an almost startled acceptance: "For the first time in my life I took a house today, and on Monday I will take possession."

From its inception as a British colony, settled under the terms of the South Australian Land Company in 1831, settlement in South Australia was intended to be regulated around the ownership of land and its productive outcomes – in ways absent from earlier settlements in older Australian colonies. But, just as had happened well before in unplanned New South Wales and Victoria, settlement got ahead of the regulations resulting in squatting and wholesale exploitation of land-sale deals. By the 1850s, there was a need to enforce the sale of pastoral tracts and farming acreages and to regulate pastoral spreads properly as pastoral leases from the Crown. The Crown Lands Consolidation Act of 1886 ushered in the wholesale oversight of land – with a Land Board – and its distribution in South Australia.

However, calls for a wider look at the taxation of property showed that calls for reform went beyond the notions of justice in the *Manifesto*. South Australia was also suffering an acute lack of revenue. Government income at the time came overwhelmingly from customs and such revenue-raising was, by the 1880s, demonstrably incapable of financing a growing population and its need for infrastructure. On 22 January 1885, the *South Australian Register* reported the regulations regarding new land taxes. Glynn's *Manifesto* was on to something. Pressure for government income from land ownership and leasing, however, would stir reactions from many in Glynn's neighbourhood.

On 10 June 1886, the *South Australian Register* reported a protest meeting at Waterloo – 40 kilometres north of Kapunda – against the South Australian land tax. At the meeting, a Mr S. Dawson – arguing for a property tax to replace the land tax – described the colony's debt as at £18,384,600 requiring a repayment annually of £761,220. This was an enormous amount. His complaint was that the government was taxing farmers too heavily to make up the deficit, while going easy on ordinary salary earners and those who lived in towns.

At the April 1887 colonial elections for South Australia, Glynn won a seat as one of two members for the electorate of Light. As he told his mother in a letter on 2 April 1887, he had won in spite of a variety of what he imagined were unpopular stances. What's more, the sitting member candidate Jenkin Coles, who led the poll, was a "formal Catholic". Glynn's election meant two Catholics had won the seat in a colony with a large Protestant majority. Surprisingly, Glynn had topped the poll in Morgan, an area wanting an irrigation scheme he had opposed. Moreover, he had argued for payment of members of parliament, without which he could not see how there would be any change to MPs being solely from the landed class and therefore no chance of reform of what he called the "landed question". But he was now elected and it had cost him £200 for a life where he would need to travel to Adelaide "3 days in the week for 5 months of the year" – something he was not looking forward to.[36]

For all that, Glynn was clearly delighted with his win, which he had only attempted, as he wrote to his mother, because "some who believed in my views pressed me to stand".[37] Coles was a tough campaigner and had treated Glynn as a competitive opponent with Glynn telling his mother, "[Coles] had me described . . . as a socialist, a revolutionist, a papist, an adventuring lawyer, an atheist, and anything else that went down."[38]

Glynn's first term as a South Australian MP was notable, but not for his ability to retain all of his supporters. As Gerald O'Collins has recorded, Glynn was far too often an independent thinker who swam against the tide. His support for free trade came as the financial downturn in South Australia made tariffs a popular policy. His support for land nationalisation and increased taxes on landowners reduced his popularity with the farming community. He even introduced a Distress for Rent Abolition Bill aimed at removing special privileges for landlords in being able to take tenants' goods in lieu of unpaid rent. The bill failed to pass. What kept his good name was his popularity as a speaker, his enduring hard work, and his integrity. Writing to his brother James in April 1888, he commented on how busy his life had become: "Every week I lecture somewhere, recently 5 nights in succession, barring Sunday. In fact, I must take the consequence of being fancied as a speaker."[39]

It came as a surprise to Glynn and his supporters that Glynn was narrowly beaten when he sought a second term at the April 1890 elections. He was popular and had served the parliament well. On 25 April, after Glynn's loss, the *South Australian Register* editorialised that "Mr Glynn's absence . . . will be a distinct loss to the House. During the three years in which he occupied a seat there he showed himself to be one of the best informed, most cultured, and most energetic of the members . . . the careful study he devoted to the questions in which he took an interest distinguished him from the rank and file representatives."

For Glynn, it was a bitter defeat as revealed in a letter to his mother on 29 April 1890, where he opined heavily: "My election was lost through, 1st bribery, 2nd Religious bigotry, because I supported the Catholic claims to school grants, 3rd misrepresentation among the ignorant German louts, of whom about 600 are on the Light Roll, 4th the treachery of my opponents."[40]

Translated, Glynn had certainly been hurt by a brutal campaign, even bribery and the buying of votes as reported on 3 May by the *Port Pirie Standard*. His upset also suggested he was still somewhat unpractised in the not-so-noble art of politics. At the declaration of the polls, the Kapunda Herald on 29 April reported Glynn as saying he "could not close his eyes to the fact that the whole of the electors had not been behaving with perfect candour, and the relations of some candidates had not acted with that candour that should exist in a democratic country". It is clear in the report that Glynn's comments were aimed squarely at his rival, Wharton White, who had taken his spot.[41] Reports of the declaration of the polls described a rowdy meeting with tense moments; many cheers for Glynn and some groans for Wharton White.

But the bitter truth was that Glynn's hard-line support for the ideas of Henry George, who happened to be on a speaking tour of South Australia that month with a visit to Kapunda included, had meant Glynn's opponent was able to smear his policies with the claim Glynn was arguing not just for land taxes but for Henry George's "single tax" – the idea that all other taxes could be replaced by one large land tax. Many in the Light electorate, "about half German" as Glynn wrote to his brother James on 6 April 1890, who were the backbone of the farming community, were not likely to take well to the thought that taxation should be levied largely, even solely, on the livelihoods of farmers.

As if to acknowledge the impact of his land nationalisation stance in the election, Glynn's editorial in the Kapunda Herald of 25 April, following the election, was a more measured look at Henry George's ideas and a distancing of Glynn from the single-tax notion. However, alongside this in the next column a report on Henry George's meeting in the Adelaide Town Hall just days before, on 21 April, set the tone for reactions to his ideas. George had a following as the meeting, which included a few wealthy squatters, revealed:

> With the exception of the greeting given to Honest Tom Playford at Norwood about a month ago, no public man had such a cheering as that which Mr George obtained when he rose to speak. Little explosions of enthusiasm interrupted the lecturer from the beginning to the ending of his philosophical discourse of an hour and three quarters duration and when the speaker sat down shortly before ten o'clock, and immediately marched off the platform with his company of single tax men, the great congregation roared forth their appreciation of his wonderful mind power until the gasoliers jingled with the atmospheric vibration.[42]

The downside for Glynn was that, in the electorate of Light, Henry George could attract a negative reaction as well. The label cast on Glynn as a single-tax man would hound him when he stood again in 1893 for Light and lost. As he wrote bitterly in his diary on 9 April 1893:

> Teutons are about 1,150 in a roll of 2,700 odd and are the chief obstacle in my way. In cranial calibre and movements they are political marionettes. They dance to the tune of their prejudices on land question, which Coles and White

everlastingly sing to them, Coles whistles nothing but single tax and strikes, and White takes up the theme with a drone about the wheat rates, the poor farmers, the land tax, and the latest local want. The idea is to lead the Germans to believe by suggestion that I am advocating the Single Tax and a fomenter of strikes.

And so it happened – as his diary recorded on 23 April 1893 – "The election was of Coles and White, the latter beating me by 1024 to 979. I expected the result and was sorry chiefly for the disappointment of my supporters." But this would not be the end of Paddy Glynn's time in the South Australian colonial parliament.

Seed time for Paddy Glynn

By 1900, Adelaide had a population of 162,000 or around a third of the population of Melbourne or Sydney. Until the drought of the 1880s coincided with the downturn in mining, South Australia had enjoyed boom times, even as the gold rushes of Victoria sapped men of working age. Wheat sales grew as the burgeoning colony of Victoria increased its imports of food and by the end of the century, South Australia was known as the 'granary of Australia'. Yet, budgets were lean by 1887 as Queen Victoria celebrated her golden jubilee. Then came the bank crashes of the 1890s, followed by depression in all Australian colonies, with South Australia being helped to stay afloat by the discovery of silver and lead at Broken Hill. At the time, Broken Hill's only rail link was with Adelaide.

With his election to the colonial parliament of South Australia, Glynn had taken to the road giving lectures while still working his legal practice, travelling hundreds of miles a week as he told his mother in a letter on 25 March 1888, "For instance, on Wednesday I drove [horse and buggy] about 75 miles, lectured and attended a ball, starting off again next morning to lecture about 150 miles nearer home." His travelling also took him to Broken Hill where he noted the opportunities for the investor or as he wrote in the same letter: "My all is in the mines, waiting for a further boom. The shares I advised John to buy are being sold at £2/10/- premium. . . . If I had the command of £1,000 two years ago, I would be worth £20,000 now. But as it is, in six months or so I may be able to clear a few thousands." Ironically, however, he would lose heavily when he sold in a panic shortly after, following poor advice from inside the government as the financial crisis took hold. Writing to his mother on 18 September he explained how he had lost, in a week, £3,500 only to find the Broken Hill mine "is better than ever and will soon pay £3 a month per share dividend".

Whether the travel had got to him or simply it was the chance to locate more centrally, in mid-1888, Glynn opened an office in Gladstone Chambers, Pirie Street, Adelaide from where he did most of his legal work. Here, he was better situated as an MP. He went to Kapunda "once a week or so" as he told his mother in the same letter. For all that his legal business was not paying hugely as times were tough. He had an apprentice, as he called his staffer, named Haurigan. For some time, he boarded on South Terrace. And then, in a matter of just two years, he was out of parliament.

For all the disappointment of his election loss, Glynn was not without public status and continued to serve on various bodies and give lectures. As he told his brother Joseph in a letter on 17 October 1890: "The *Kapunda Herald* articles – 2 a week – keep my hand in and pay for hunters [horses], and invitations to lecture come in pairs. Though not in Parliament, I am still a member of Royal Commissions. Yesterday I was chosen one of three to go to Victoria and NSW to try and settle, or bring about a conference to settle, inter-colonial River questions. Had I been in Parliament this time, I would have been appointed to the Australasian Convention to draw up the Federal Constitution – but the Gods will otherwise, or rather the beery electors."[43]

Glynn's recreational interest in riding kept him in better spirits. He had a new mare, whom he named Modesty, and who was showing outstanding talent for the steeplechase, although, as he told his mother on 25 August 1890, the horse was "excitable" and had bolted as a cab of women crossed their path, causing a smash from which, Glynn recorded, all "luckily found ourselves on this side of eternity". Horses were keeping him going in this political downtime – as he told his brother Joseph in the same letter: "The [cost of] elections almost crippled me, but I value life little now, and as long as I can keep a hunter to carry me over 1,000 4 feet solid fences per season, I can drag on."

There was another factor in Glynn's ability to persist, found in his love of literature and reading. In his letter of 25 August 1890 to his mother, he professed: "I don't mind bad luck, especially as really the best world to live in is one of thought." The Glynn brothers also shared an intellectual ambience. James had just produced a new novel. Joseph had sent Glynn his essay on Burke, whom Glynn wrote back to saying it gave him "pleasure" and adding: "Like Carlyle he is one that cannot be imitated, but there is a Miltonic grandeur of diction and thought about Burke that elevates the reader." It was seed time again for Paddy Glynn. And the age was moving in his direction as matters of federation came into focus. Glynn may not have been a delegate at the 1890 Australasian Convention to draw up a federal constitution but that meeting was just the beginning of far more complex discussions and practical debates in the years to come. And Glynn was already forming his arguments for the new democratic system about to unfold.

Undoubtedly, it was the writings of Edmund Burke, the father of modern conservatism, which most often inspired Patrick McMahon Glynn. Glynn took from Burke his support for trade liberalisation, due process, and constitutional protections, as well as his distrust of big and over bureaucratised government. And he cheered Burke's stance on the American colonies' uprising against the British. Writing to his brother Joseph in March 1892, he reflected, "The great Edmund was at his best when he championed the cause of the colonists. He was wiser than his hearers and more liberal than his clients." In his speech on Edmund Burke for the Irish National Federation on 15 November 1897, Glynn extolled Burke's achievements. *The Advertiser* on 16 November reported Glynn assessing Burke's writings on the American Revolution:

> He cared nothing for mere abstract right when in politics it was opposed to, in the higher sense, expediency and convenience. He urged Parliament, while declaring the right to impose them, to repeal the duties. "Great and acknowledged force," he said, "is not impaired either in effect or opinion by an unwillingness to exert itself. The superior power may offer peace with honour and with safety. . . . We cannot, I fear, falsify the pedigree of this fierce people and persuade them that they are not sprung from a nation in whose veins the blood of freedom circulates."[44]

Yet, while admitting that "Burke was right", Glynn assessed the majority of the colonists in revolt against the British as having been given a spirit by history "they never possessed". According to Glynn, "It was the absence, under the Confederation Arrangement, of an Executive capable of compelling the States to send in their contributions, that showed the Statesmen of the Revolution the utter impossibility of getting on without complete Federation."[45]

In his editorial of 22 July 1890 in the *Kapunda Herald*, Glynn laid out his views on the lessons of history as to be found in the American War of Independence and the constitution that followed. For Glynn, Washington had led a mixed bag of mostly self-interested colonists, albeit founding a great democracy:

> The members who composed that over which Washington presided looked upon the business of federation as one chiefly of profit and loss, cared little about prestige, and took nothing for granted except that it was expedient to quarrel. For all its great and beneficent effect upon the growth of the Anglo-Celtic race, the American revolution was carried by the selfishness of the many and the patriotism of the few. . . But for the ever-active and self-sacrificing genius of Washington, and the contemptible incapacity of Howe and Cornwallis, their desertions in moments of doubt and danger would have led to a different issue of contest.

To Glynn, as it would appear to the founding fathers generally, the shape of the Australian federation would be balanced against the flaws and strengths of those founded before. At the Adelaide federation convention, Glynn voiced his reservations about the motivations of earlier federations across the globe:

The American Union was, in its primary objects, a defensive alliance – the issue of fear; begotten of sense of danger from isolation and diversity, and a keen consciousness of necessity in the struggle for life. Stripped of the romance of rebellion and the glamour of success the movement which was crowned with the Constitution of 1787, was not the outcome of a wild and ennobling impulse of patriotism, a fight for a great ideal [but] the method of commonplace and calculating men, of commercial instincts and narrow ambitions. . . . The Swiss Federation was not the product of a splendid foresight and love, but the fruit of 600 years of dissension and dangers.[46]

Concluding his editorial of 22 July 1890, Glynn had high hopes that in the rational and peaceful world of the Australian colonies, a federation could be achieved from the best of the precedents to be found in others: "These and other conditions of federal Government have to be studied by those who would strike a fair balance of the merits and drawbacks of the system." He continued to hold this optimistic view in 1897, telling the Adelaide Convention: "[Ours] is the creation of desire, the product of prudence and passion – of passion for the larger life and nobler aims, and that can build before the breaking of the storm."[47]

Political groupings resembling political parties were barely beginning in the 1890s in the Australian colonies. After losing Light a second time, Glynn noted in his diary for 23 April 1893 that "Labor, for the first time, has a good representation in the Assembly – 8 out of 54 – I see no reason to regret the fact." Groupings around personalities and issues were more the order of the day.

Glynn kept at his legal work, the earnings from which were

meagre. With his move to Adelaide in 1888 and his days in Kapunda reduced, his time at the Kapunda Herald came to an end in 1891. As he wrote to his sister Elizabeth on 27 November 1894, "Times are very bad here. I could do with two clerks, & have to keep three or throw one fellow's mother on her uppers, as they say. I get nine Counsels' work but there is little cash about. In getting the Rodney men off at Broken Hill for burning a vessel, I scored well, making the best speech of my life." Glynn's biographer, Gerald O'Collins, regarded this win as a highlight of his grandfather's time at the bar.[48]

With the death of George Charles Hawker, member for North Adelaide, in June 1895, Glynn's political career returned. Urged to stand for the seat, Glynn was courted by the fledgling Labor groups. Although Glynn considered making Labor his flag, he chose otherwise with a preference for retaining his independence. Possibly, the visit of Irish Nationalist MP Michael Davitt, supported by the Trades and Labour Council in Adelaide, due around the time of the by-election, influenced Glynn's thinking. Davitt was a supporter of Henry George and the idea of the single tax. Glynn was happy to praise Davitt for his work "to break down prejudices between Ireland and England by placing them on a common platform of democratic opinion" but preferred to see his support was separate from any connection to a particular group. [49] As Gerald O'Collins acknowledges, Glynn also had differences with Labor on a number of its policies.[50]

Glynn won the by-election for Hawker's seat of North Adelaide only to lose it the following year and win it back in another by-election in 1887. He retained the seat at the 1899 election and was Attorney-General in the very brief (seven-day) Solomon Ministry. It would not, however, be the end of

Glynn's career in politics. In 1897, Glynn was one of ten South Australian delegates elected as representatives at the Federation Conventions to be held in Adelaide, Sydney, and Melbourne.

A nation comes together

The vision of a united continent of Australia was not new in the 1890s. The notion went back to an 1847 initiative proposed by the Colonial Secretary, Earl Grey, for a General Assembly acting as a central authority across the Australian colonies. Various proposals were ventured over successive decades. New South Wales's Henry Parkes would emerge as the father of an Australian federation in the last decades of the nineteenth century. As Helen Irving has pointed out, "the 1880s would prove the turning point at which the 'federal idea' (found in all schemes of the previous forty years) would be transformed into the Federation movement."[51] The Federal Council of Australia Act was passed by the parliament at Westminster in August 1885, permitting all colonies to confer bi-annually on actions and legislation beneficial to the common Australasian interest. However, the matter of defence of the Australian colonies was the foremost issue compelling the colonies to think of united action. In his Tenterfield Oration in 1889, Henry Parkes pushed for a federal meeting on such a question. Hence, the eventual National Australasian Convention of 1891 held in Sydney.

The convention of 1891 achieved little progress to a federal constitution but the Federal Council continued to meet and federation leagues sprang up. At the premiers' conference in January 1895, plans for a new federal convention were set in place. In early 1897, ten delegates from each of four colonies were elected – the West Australian government chose to nominate its own ten delegates and Queensland remained unrepresented. Helen Irving has described what followed: "These fifty men then met on 22 March that year and, during sessions lasting several weeks at a time, up to 17 March 1898, they debated and conferred and drafted, and finally came up with a new Constitution for the Commonwealth of Australia."[52]

The Adelaide convention assembled in what is now the west wing of the South Australian Parliament on North Terrace, completed in 1889. The chamber with its colonnades at the Speaker's end and dark heavy drapes separating large portraits of colonial leaders on both side walls was fitted with three rows of members' seats facing each other with a wide space between at the end of which – in front of the Speaker's chair – was a large table for clerks. The packed public gallery high above the Speaker's chair looked out over a strange collection of dark crimson drapes falling in waves from the ceiling, designed to improve the quality of sound below in these days without microphones. Between the drapes hung gaslight chandeliers (gasoliers) to brighten this windowless room.[53]

In becoming a delegate to the conventions that led to Australian federation, Glynn would find more self-interest than he bargained for among the colonists. Alfred Deakin, in *The Federal Story*, described many personal and political divisions among the delegates of the federation conventions:

> In New South Wales the three ministers, Reid, Carruthers and Brunker, cherished some resentment towards Barton, Lyne and O'Connor, the Protectionist leaders of the local Opposition. . . . Reid could not forget that although Premier of New South Wales he held but second place to Barton in the national poll, watching events with an

evident determination to attain what he considered his due position in the Convention. In South Australia party lines were drawn with absolute distinctness – Kingston, Holder, Cockburn as Ministers and Gordon as their late colleague on the one side with Baker. Symon, Downer, Howe, Solomon and less aggressively Glynn on the other. Not only was political passion strong in all, but personal antipathies were violent. Kingston once challenged Baker to a duel and had been arrested walking with a loaded revolver in his pocket at the part of the public street which he had named as place of meeting.[54]

And that was just New South Wales and South Australia. For all that, Deakin attested that "the members worked amicably and in all the five [colonies] party differences were at once sunk upon any provincial issue or upon any truly national question".

While the debates at the federation conventions of 1897 and 1898 settled to a working arrangement, soon enough, the early reports for the first meeting in Adelaide suggested acrimony and division early on stood out as a problem in such a momentous undertaking. As reflected in the editorial of the *South Australian Register*, on 24 March 1897, it took time to settle differences for the bigger issue:

"A cloudy morning" sometimes "brings a perfect day"; but at other times the dawn murk is only the precursor of storm. The Federation Convention may end satisfactorily, but it has not opened auspiciously. On the very first day of its meeting there were suppressed signs of friction which . . . has not since decreased; and though a little misunderstanding may be only natural in the circumstances, it may develop into something worse unless the representatives of the various colonies keep themselves well under restraint.

Delegates soon rose to the occasion, however. Another report of the opening day in the Melbourne *Argus* on 23 March showed that, as delegates took on board the seriousness of the assembly, the need to find unity of purpose became obvious as the delegates caucused to decide on a president for the convention. The outcome was the choice of South Australia's premier, Charles Kingston, with delegates from Victoria and New South Wales urging unity and with Victorian delegates, Alfred Deakin and Billy Trenwith, warning "that to have a conflict in open convention at its very first sitting would tend to belittle the importance of the gathering in the eyes of the public."[55]

Sharp differences of perspective and colonial self-interest would underpin the delegates' discourse and debate over those two years. The three federation conventions of 1897-98, the colonial referenda, and the negotiations with Britain that followed finally brought the six colonies of Australia to federate in 1901. It was indeed a herculean achievement. In arriving at this outcome, various movements and radical ideas underpinned the view that a new nation might be conceived.

Much of this centred on fresh expressions of identity such as the nationalism reflected in *The Bulletin* and the Australian Natives Association, and even the new cultural voice of Australian literature in the writings of the likes of Henry Lawson and Banjo Paterson, developing a notion that there was something intrinsically Australian after all. The bush theme became sentimentalised, unifying what was essentially a collection of urban settlements. Alongside that were the utopian imaginings and experiments of radicals such as William Lane and his New Australia in Paraguay, but also a number of local communal-style settlements begun with government support in the 1890s. For example, Charles Kingston's South Australian government established co-operative settlements on the Murray River intending to alleviate unemployment by taking up utopian ideas to be found in the labour movement. Above and beyond all this was the ever-pressing feeling that not just defence but also immigration needed a united effort to ensure the living standards of a 'white' and British settlement would not be swamped by outsiders in the form of Asian or Pacific cheap labour.

Into this milieu came Paddy Glynn – the litterateur of the old country but of Irish descent. A man who read copiously from the past in the English tradition albeit with traces of the agitator from his adherence to the protests of the Irish Land League and his support for Irish Home Rule. But also, an immigrant who had made his home in the Australian colonies and one who, in spite of eventually being able to afford the journey, would return only once to his birth country. Patrick McMahon Glynn would seal his impact on the conventions in a number of ways – for his eloquence and erudition certainly, but also for his contribution on the divided issue of water rights across the Murray-Darling basin, for the insertion of a reference to Almighty God in the preamble to the Constitution, his support for free trade between the colonies as States, and his tireless opposition to creating institutional bodies that would expand the costs of a new federal system while merely duplicating the work of the States.

Glynn's seductive eloquence made its mark in the first days of the Adelaide convention, alongside his erudition and wealth of knowledge. A cameo of Patrick McMahon Glynn at the first convention was recorded in Sydney's *Daily Telegraph* on 25 March 1897:

From right away at the back benches a diminutive figure,

41

in a brown tweed suit and a light blue necktie, sprang up and caught the President's attention. This was Mr Glynn. . . . In a few seconds he had drenched the Convention in a torrent of words. . . . He favoured a Federal judiciary, and distinctly affirmed in favour of the consolidation of the national debts. Not that he thought for one moment that unification of the stock would give the world any greater idea of the solvency of the colonies, because financiers knew that already. . . . He contemptuously dashed aside the fears expressed by Sir Richard Baker as to the system of responsible government under Federation and quoted learned authorities who had an implicit belief in genus of the English system. . . . Mr Glynn had volumes, documents, papers and reports, and from one he travelled to another. He quoted extensively. He threw masses of statistics at the representatives. He went to the United States, to Germany, to Austria. Words still poured out in a continuous and a magnificent stream. . . . Mr Glynn took his seat amid general cheering.[56]

God and the Constitution

If eloquence and presentation underpinned Glynn's rather thespian appeal, in spite of the speed at which he spoke and his heavy Irish accent, the use of words and their significance were just as important to him. On 22 April 1897, Glynn put a motion to the Adelaide convention that would define his part in the federation agreement. As Alfred Deakin and Edmund Barton concluded a somewhat pedantic discussion to change the word "form" to "unite in", Glynn rose to propose a more significant amendment of words:

> I have an amendment which I move, not on my own unsupported initiative, but at the suggestion of other members of this Convention. It is: That before the word

"have" on the second line of the preamble the words "invoking Divine Providence" be inserted.[57]

He went on to explain that many groups of citizens had requested the added reference he was suggesting: ". . . we cannot pass over in silence the almost unanimous request of the members of so many creeds, of one aim and hope, that the Supremacy of God should be recognised, and His blessing invoked in the opening lines of our Constitution."[58] He added, "The foundations of our national edifice are being laid in times of peace; the invisible hand of Providence is in the tracing of our plans. Should we not, at the very inception of our great work, give some outward recognition of the Divine guidance that we feel?"[59]

For the era, it should not have been odd that a delegate would propose such an inclusion of reference to God in the Constitution's preamble.* And Glynn was confident the proposal fitted with the ambience of Australia as a British settlement. "Says Burke," he assured the delegates, "we know, and, what is better, we feel inwardly that religion is the basis of civil society." For, as he put it, "It is felt in the forms of our courts of justice, in the language of our Statutes, in the oath that binds the sovereign to the observance of our liberties, the recognition of the Sabbath, in the rubrics of our guilds and social orders, in the anthem through which on every public occasion we invoke a blessing on our executive head."[60] Glynn often questioned the rubrics of his faith but, like his hero, Edmund Burke, never the wider influence of Christian belief on the stability of civil society.

---

* The reference to Almighty God is in fact contained in the preamble to the Commonwealth of Australia Constitution Act 1900. This is an enactment of the Parliament at Westminster. The Act empowered Queen Victoria to issue a proclamation declaring that the people of the Australian colonies would be united in a Federal Commonwealth, and that the Constitution of that Commonwealth would take the form set out in the Act. The Constitution itself does not contain a preamble of any sort.

As the delegates argued the proposal, it became clear that Glynn had a perception of God as something beyond personal faith in any particular denomination. His God was a universal spirit that linked mankind in metaphysical ways. Alan Atkinson, in *The Europeans in Australia*, writes of Glynn's God as "ubiquitous and vast" or the "creative effort about something immeasurable", adding:

> He was trying to find words which might express ancient but still living habits of association, not state-of-the-art statistical analysis. He wanted a reminder as to what the people did among themselves, how they existed among themselves, as a body. Glynn spoke . . . [of] a spirit moving through nations, guiding people . . . to higher things. Glynn's God surfaces in innumerable small phenomena, eternal but ephemeral.[61]

Indeed, those who were opposing Glynn's proposal could not see past the sectarian issues that had defined much of the education debate in the colonies over the decades before. That debate had offered secular education as the only education supported by any government's financial contribution. But the motion put by Glynn was, at the same time, pushed by a flood of petitions: on the first day, seven petitions signed by over 17,000; over the next three days, another sixteen more containing some 140,000 signatures. And they kept coming. As Christian Bergmann has argued, Glynn was "responding to a tension that was already existing and had defined political debate in Australian colonial politics throughout the course of the federal movement. It was a tension between the idealism of nationalism and the material, economic interests that each of the colonies were pursuing."[62]

The immediate reaction of opposition to Glynn's proposal

would have surprised him. Tasmanian delegate 81-year-old Adye Douglas, a lawyer of Scottish birth who held the view that prayers in the House of Commons were "a farce", began his response by suggesting Glynn's "sermon" would have been of much interest if "given in another place". Edmund Barton, who would become Australia's first prime minister, followed next with further objections to which Sir Edward Braddon from Tasmania offered his "Hear, Hear". Barton went on to put strong arguments that the insertion of such a phrase in the Constitution would jeopardise long-held notions of a separation of church and state in constitutional matters: "The whole duty is to render unto Caesar the things that are Caesar's and unto God the things that are God's."[63]

It was left to delegate James Walker, a banker from New South Wales, to intervene and support Glynn's reference to petitions from citizens – he had received a petition from several thousand inhabitants of New South Wales. He also reminded delegates that, at the beginning of the convention, they had received a telegram from the Secretary of State for the Colonies, on behalf of the Queen, which alluded to the guidance of Divine Providence. And he added that delegates who were absent on this day – George Reid (premier of New South Wales), Sir Joseph Abbott, and a colleague of Reid, Joseph Carruthers – had said they would support the motion. By this time, however, the strong opposition of Barton seems to have left Glynn thinking his motion was unsettling and he offered to withdraw it.[64] But Sir George Turner objected saying this would not be a good look in that it would appear the convention had unanimously rejected the idea. A vote was taken, and the motion was lost 17 votes to 11.

A reference to the Divine in the preamble to the Constitution would ultimately win the day at the Melbourne sitting of the convention on 2 March 1898. It was the culmination of a grassroots campaign by churches of all denominations, eventually supported by nine of the ten colonial houses of parliament in the five colonies represented. Detailed accounts of the campaign and its success can be found in Gerald O'Collins's *Patrick McMahon Glynn: A Founder of Federation* and in Frank Brennan's essay, "A History of Respectful Debate" in *Today's Tyrants: Responding to Dyson Heydon*, edited by Damien Freeman.

After Glynn's motion was lost in Adelaide, some Protestant collectives gave voice to the criticism that Glynn himself was the reason for the failure. Dr John Laurence Rentoul, of Ormond College in Melbourne, vented his displeasure at Glynn at the Presbyterian Assembly in May 1897, accusing Glynn of not going about his motion "in the proper way". For Rentoul, Glynn was "a young Roman Catholic barrister" who had caused "mischief".[65] As Rentoul saw it, there should have been a concerted campaign to persuade the delegates before the motion had been put. Such criticism served only to expose sectarian divides and did little to help the cause.

In fact, in spite of the voluminous nature of the petitions, overwhelmingly from Christian churches, no campaign had been organised by the church groups themselves. With the defeat of the motion, campaigns formed, as did unity of purpose. Eventually, it became a force for persuading colonial parliaments that some reference to God in the Constitution was needed. By the time of the Melbourne convention in early 1898, it was becoming evident to many delegates that, if a vote was to be won to bring federation about, the insertion of a reference to God would be in the interests of one and all, not just Christian believers. On 2 March, Glynn moved that the words "humbly relying on the blessing of Almighty God" should be inserted into the preamble. He continued:

> I wish to move the insertion of this form of words in the preamble, because I think that it embodies the spirit of the nine suggestions in regard to this matter made by the various Houses of Parliament which have considered the Draft Constitution. The words I wish to insert are simple and unsectarian. They are expressive of our ultimate hope of the final end of all our aspirations, of the great elemental truth upon which all our creeds are based, and towards which the lines of our faiths converge. They will, I think, recommend the Constitution to thousands to whom the rest of its provisions may for ever be a sealed book.[66]

The motion put by Glynn was eventually agreed to without a vote. However, in disagreeing with the insertion of the words referencing Almighty God, delegate Henry Bournes Higgins argued, "I should have no objection to the insertion of words of this kind in the preamble, if I felt that in the Constitution we had a sufficient safeguard against the passing of religious laws by the Commonwealth." He did not, however, believe there was such a safeguard. Other delegates argued similar reservations. Frank Brennan has written, "It's not that they were concerned about the right of citizens to enjoy freedom of religion or freedom from religion. They simply saw religion and its public manifestations and limitations as matters for the States and not the Commonwealth."[67]

Having accepted that Glynn's words "humbly relying on the blessing of Almighty God" be inserted into the preamble, later that day Higgins pushed for the acceptance of a further amendment in order to safeguard the rights of the States to make laws relating to religion. He moved: ". . . the insertion of the following new clause to replace clause 109 already struck out: 'The Commonwealth shall not make any law prohibiting the free exercise of any religion, or for the establishment of any religion, or imposing any religious observance, and no religious test shall be required as a qualification for any office or public trust under the Commonwealth.'"[68] This would go on to form the basis of section 116 of the Constitution:

> The Commonwealth shall not make any law for establishing any religion, or for imposing any religious observance, or for prohibiting the free exercise of any religion, and no religious test shall be required as a qualification for any office or public trust under the Commonwealth.

In their desire to protect the right of the States to legislate on laws relating to religion, the convention delegates wished only to preserve the separation of church and state as to be found in the American Constitution. That being so, it is now ironic that echoes of Glynn and reactions to his motion have returned to the federal government as it responds to the *Religious Freedom Review* in the wake of changes to the *Marriage Act* in 2017. With the new laws accepting same-sex marriage in Australia – laws under the federal jurisdiction – problems have emerged for church or religious run institutions where religious tenets now conflict with legal realities.

As Greg Craven outlined in an article for *The Australian* on 5 January 2019, there are hidden traps for religious bodies in simply carrying on according to their faith and beliefs: "To make matters even more complicated, the law dealing with the permitted scope of religious preaching and teaching mainly is contained in various state discrimination and anti-discrimination statutes, with only the odd mention in federal legislation."[69] As the federal government, either Labor or Coalition, seeks to address the problems that have now arisen for religious freedom from the 2017 changes to the Marriage Act, by involving itself in matters Section 116 intended to protect as a States only issue – some of the warnings of 1897 and 1898 at the federation conventions will come back to haunt it. Thanks to Patrick McMahon Glynn and the people who supported his motion, the blessing of Almighty God may well be needed.

Love and marriage – for Delegate Glynn

The Sydney sittings of the federation conventions were held between 2-24 September 1897. Glynn, as a distinguished former MP from South Australia who had worked for committees and the government, was a much-travelled Australian by the standards of the times. That he had still not married may have mystified some. Reading his diaries, however, it is obvious that Glynn had settled into a work-dominated routine and that, moreover, routine was an important part of his life. His love of reading saw him happy to pass hours alone, although he did enjoy company if there was the stimulation of argument and conversation. His endless invitations to give speeches to clubs and societies also made him available to a wide assortment of people. That he remained single at the age of forty-two was also no longer a matter of lacking the necessary finances.

Glynn's reticent emotional life when it came to marriage is explained by Gerald O'Collins as emanating both from his relationship with his mother, which was always intellectual and unemotional, and from the fact that he wanted to marry a Catholic. In South Australia, where Catholics were but one-in-eight of the population, few were found among Glynn's social class. Writing to his mother after his brother Joseph's marriage, on 16 July 1895, Glynn mused, "I suppose Joseph is quite settled down now. I wish I was, but coreligionists here are not a polished lot. I never – almost never – meet a Catholic at a dance."[70]

However, at the second federal convention in Sydney, Glynn found the moment. It produced newsworthy circumstances. On Tuesday, 7 September 1897 and in the midst of days of debates about matters constitutional, Glynn sent a rather long-winded letter of proposal to 29-year-old Abigail Dynon, the beautiful daughter of Melbourne's John and Abigail Dynon, immigrants from Ireland who had made their fortune in a china business. Glynn and Abigail had met just once a year or so before. Glynn had made some flippant comment on marriage and asked her to "wait for him". She had indeed. Abigail accepted the proposal by telegram and Glynn left the conference that Friday travelling by train to Melbourne where the couple were married the next day, with King O'Malley as best man.

Gerald O'Collins writes of Glynn's absence of an emotional relationship with his mother: "This childhood lack readily explains why he would marry so late, and then choose a girl whom he barely knew and to whom he could scarcely have any strong emotional attachment."[71] Thus, surrounded by delegates and their diaries full of public functions, Abigail and Glynn began what would prove to be a most successful union. Nearly two decades later, in 1915, Tasmanian treasurer and future Australian prime minister, Joseph Lyons, would match the

Glynn honeymoon by taking his seventeen-year-old bride, Enid, to Sydney for a premiers' conference.

Adjustment to married status was gradual for Glynn, as was fatherhood. For some time in rare mentions of Abigail in his diary, Glynn spoke of her only as "wife" – as in his entry for 18 April 1898: "On Thursday I went to Melbourne to fetch my wife back. She remained after the end of the Convention until after Easter." Or, for 5 August 1898: "About dawn this morning the wife gave birth to a son." No further comment. Family details were still at a minimum five years later: "Sunday, 8 October 1904: On Wednesday . . . I spoke on the no-confidence motion, criticising the Labor party for having attenuated their policy with a view to power and condemning the wholesale condemnation of socialism; and Mrs Glynn had a son. The Speech, according to members and some press-men who spoke to me, was effective."

Over the years, in his diary, Glynn could wax lyrical about romance, the poets, and love in the abstract. Yet, some inner constraint cautioned record of the truly personal and emotional. Even for the christening of his first child on 18 August 1898: "The youngster was christened, John, yesterday at North Adelaide Church, Father Adamson being the Celebrant. His Aunt, Mary Dynon, and Dan Dynon (in absentia) stood for him. Basil Dynon, his youngest Uncle on his mother's side, was also present and is here tonight. A dog, Irish terrier, arrived from Melbourne by rail today."

It would be different for Glynn, however, as he recorded in his diary the sudden death of little John on 21 February 1899: "Our dear little child is dead. He was on Thursday morning apparently well, except for teething troubles, but he suddenly, while in his mother's arms, changed his expression from that look of wonder and enquiry, which seldom passed into anything but a bright little smile, and within a few minutes was lost to us . . . it is something (for me) to have been bettered in heart by his little life, and to have felt what a child is or may be when he first begins to notice. It is well his mother has the steadfast faith which alone can render the loss, at her age, of a first-born bearable."[72]

Political life would be the dominant force in the Glynn household over the decades. While a devoted parent and husband, Glynn spent many weeks away from his home. Abigail was the perfect partner in this, managing the domestic scene and spending a lot of time with her own family in Melbourne where the federal parliament sat in the years Glynn was a Member. The family grew quickly, with Glynn jotting in his diary for 15 June 1902, "Another daughter born on Wednesday 11th June. I was at the time in Melbourne. Joan [born 1899] was the first to announce the event on my return." The McMahon Glynns were by then parents of three daughters, and would have a total of eight children between 1898 and 1912 – three sons and five daughters with their firstborn John dying at barely six months and daughter Alice, in 1906, dying within days of her birth. Family summers were spent at the seaside in Adelaide and Glynn diarised that his public life was at many times no pleasure and he ached for the regularity and familiarity of his home. Writing to his sister Agnes on 27 October 1912, Glynn gave something of the busy schedule he had developed:

> What a domestic life a Federal Public man has! In months
> I have not had more than a weekend at home. As I write
> the children are in bed. Abbie and Mary are in Melbourne,
> staying with Mary Dynon. I seldom see them when there as

I stay at a hotel. We may rise before Christmas; but I return
to clear out to the seaside for the children's holidays.[73]

In Glynn's unemotional style, life barely skipped a beat as
he settled down as a married man. He had chosen well, and his
regular and ordered lifestyle continued in many ways much as
it has always been. But, as he admitted in his diary entry at the
death of his firstborn in February 1899, he had "been bettered in
heart" by the attachments of family and married life.

The federal politician

On Monday, 1 April 1901, *The Advertiser* announced the results
of the first (state-wide) federal election for South Australia
including the report that "Mr Glynn who enjoys a uniform
popularity throughout the State, stands fourth on the list."
He was actually third on the list of seven for South Australia.
Having raised his profile through the federation conventions,
by the time of the first election for the federal parliament in
1901 Glynn had been elected as one of the seven MPs for South
Australia. South Australia and Tasmania conducted their 1901
elections much like today's Senate, with candidates being
chosen by the whole of the State. When South Australians went
to the election of 1903, there were by then seven new federal
electorates and Glynn would be returned unopposed as the
Member for Angus.

The federal parliament would sit in Melbourne until the
opening of Parliament House, Canberra, in 1927. Glynn would
hold his seat for almost two decades until 1919. He would be the
last of the founding fathers to remain in the federal parliament
and was present at the opening of the new Parliament House in
Canberra in 1927. Glynn, like all the Founding Fathers of the

Australian Commonwealth, would never sit in the parliament in Canberra.

Glynn's diary entries for 1900-01 indicate that he was a close observer of the political jockeying from the start, leaving Adelaide on Christmas Day 1900 for Sydney to join in the celebrations and consultations around the first ministry. Glynn was, at the time, regarded as the unofficial deputy to New South Wales Free Trader George Reid, who headed what would become the main opposition to Edmund Barton and Alfred Deakin's Protectionists. Reid asked him to canvass Western Australia for the Free Traders in the coming elections. Of the backroom 'negotiations', Glynn wrote in his diary for 4 January 1901, "The secret history of the canvassing for the Premiership and positions in the Cabinet would probably not show some of those concerned in the best of lights. There is a general sense that the offices and posts had been bespoken beforehand by [a] political syndicate of which Barton, Deakin, Kingston, and probably Turner (but that is doubtful) were the chief shareholders and directors."

For all that, an earnest desire to be part of public endeavour pushed him on. His entry for 17 May 1903 includes the following observation: "But we stick to Politics, with its distractions, vulgarities, trickeries, and compensating preferments only for the few, either as an outlet for unexercised energies or giving scope for the prompting of an empty ambition."

Within months of taking his seat in the federal parliament, the Immigration Restriction Bill, which would usher in the White Australia Policy to restrict the entry of 'aliens' to Australia, was debated in the House of Representatives. Glynn made his very unique contribution on 6 September 1901, arguing against suggestions from the British Secretary of State for the Colonies, Joseph Chamberlain, that Australia should not offend Asian nations such as China and Japan by legislation excluding "aliens" (read Asians) and instead exclude prospective immigrants who were "dirty, or paupers, or immoral". For Glynn, this was an "egregious piece of moral cant". As he saw it:

> So far as men being paupers is concerned, we have to recollect that some of the best men – men of enterprise, men of intelligence, men through whom the British Empire has become what it is – landed on these shores practically stone broke. They were not what we know as paupers within the meaning of an Act of Parliament, but there were very few men who landed here, stirred by a desire to take part in the development of this great country, who landed here with more than a few pounds in their pockets; and are we going to leave it to some subordinate officer of the Executive to determine what degree of poverty shall afford justification for the exclusion of an immigrant?

He had equal mockery for suggestions that regulatory officers might inspect any prospective immigrant's morality. For all that, Glynn accepted that Australian workers' wages needed protection from the import of cheap labour, even as he continued to argue that there was no dramatic influx of Chinese in Australia at that time.

Regular themes in speeches Glynn made from 1901 were opposition to big government and protection of industries. His view that the federal government needed to be wary of taking on a larger role in the administration of areas that overlapped States' responsibilities could be found in his objection to added bureaucracy in the form of interstate commissions. "The position I take," he told the House, on 7 November 1901, while arguing against the setting up of an inter-State railways commission, "is that any machinery not really required for the purposes of the Constitution should not be created. I look upon all political machinery as more or less an evil."

On the issue of the establishment of a High Court, likewise, Glynn argued that there was little need to set up an entirely separate legal jurisdiction. In the first years of the Commonwealth, many could not imagine what matters might justify the expense of such a body. He argued that the Commonwealth needed to "proceed slowly" and until the federal government was more developed, and that Sir Samuel Griffith's suggestion for an appellate court made up of State judges should be adopted.[74]

With the Second Reading of the Judiciary Bill on 9 June 1903, Glynn argued in the House: "If the Bill passes as it stands, it will bring about centralisation in original Federal matters, will entail very great expense upon litigants, and probably crush out those who are poor." And in response to Alfred Deakin, justifying the Bill on account of his belief that "the Federal Constitution, and the laws under it, will create a great number of appeals", Glynn retorted, "If that be so, I wish the electors had been informed of the fact prior to the referendum being taken. If they had imagined that the product of Federation would be an increase in the amount of litigation, I venture to believe that they would have hesitated before voting in favour of Federal union."

In a diary entry for 28 June 1903, Glynn wrote, "I led the opposition in Committee to the Judiciary Bill. We have practically made it a Court of Appeal of three judges, by preventing any additions to the original jurisdiction given by the Constitution. My object is to prevent the Electoral mind being offended by the play of too much, and unnecessary, machinery in the early days of Federation." In time, Glynn not only accepted the High Court, but appeared in cases before it. Today, over a century later, Glynn would be stunned to see the increased breadth of Commonwealth powers – largely awarded by High Court decisions – and its commissions.

In the matter of protection and tariffs, Glynn believed the hand of what today we would call the 'nanny state' was a hindrance to healthy growth. His dislike of any form of unlevel playing field in trade included a strong opposition to what was then called 'Imperial preference', whereby the nations of the British Empire gave preference to each other in matters of trade. As he told the House on 10 December 1901, in response to argument from Victorian Protectionist Isaac Isaacs, "The honourable and learned member would put straps around the waist of every industry and keep it on crutches until the day of doom. The old idea was that it was sufficient to extend protection to infant industries for about fifteen years, but the modern idea is to keep them infants forever."

The political groupings in the first decade of the Commonwealth parliament evolved in rather fluid ways. When Alfred Deakin's Protectionist Ministry was defeated on 21 April 1904, over its inability to pass the Arbitration Bill, Labor formed its first Ministry with Labor's leader Chris Watson briefly serving as Prime Minister. Like Labor, Glynn had opposed the Arbitration Bill, not necessarily for the same reasons but he was sympathetic to some of Labor's positions. Glynn's diary, for 24 April 1904, records that he was approached by two Labor MPs who, he wrote, "would have been glad to have me as Attorney-General – if I would accept". Glynn declined.

Meanwhile, the Free Trade Party's George Reid was making

overtures to his opponents in the Protectionist group to try and form a coalition with a chance the Governor-General might call him. Glynn and a handful of the Reid group, as Glynn's diary recorded on 24 April, "released him" and expressed "a reserve of judgement as to future action". But the Governor-General called for Watson. Then, in August, the Watson Ministry fell, and Reid was called after managing to form a coalition from remnants of the Deakin group. On 21 August, Glynn wrote in his diary:

> Reid has formed a Ministry, taking in his deputy in the Free Trade opposition, Dugald Thompson, Sydney Smith his Whip and Symon, the generally absent and therefore nominal leader of the Once Free Trade party of the Senate. Turner, M'Lean, M'Cay represent Victoria and protection, though protection is chiefly of personal interests. Reid has shown himself a man of little political principle or consistency and his Whip, Sydney Smith, outside the question of free trade, of still less. Both supported the Arbitration Bill.

Glynn was not playing hardliner in this, having watched Reid sell out the Protectionists to gain the premiership. He could in fact bend initial stances when convinced of the need to change. Glynn had opposed the colonies' support for the war in the Sudan in 1885, editorialising in the *Kapunda Herald* that jingoism had forced the British government's hand in its decision to send troops and that, "The saner mind of England has been consciously infected by the temper of the delirious rabble and out of reference to the latter, closes its eye upon its own reasoning and takes up the cry of prestige."[75] Likewise, at the start of Britain's conflict with the Boers in South Africa, Glynn was initially against support for Britain and Australian colonies sending troops. Then, his views changed to believe it was a "duty" to the Empire for the Australian colonies to commit forces to the South African campaign, even as he commented in his diary on 21 January 1900, how he feared the jingoism the war had caused.[76] When the new federal parliament eventually agreed to send more Australian troops to South Africa, Glynn spoke in the House, on 14 January 1902, to condemn the "timidity and vacillation" of the Barton Ministry in the delay of its decision to raise the contingent. However, by the time the Australian troops arrived in South Africa, the war had ended.

By August 1904, it was the opportunism of Reid – the mark of a lot of successful politicians – that galled Glynn. Deakin, in many respects, now represented Glynn's idea of a principled politician. Unlike Reid, Deakin preferred to remain in opposition than do a deal to form a government. Ironically, Glynn would be given his first ministerial position – as Attorney-General – in the Deakin Ministry of 1909-10.

As the federal parliament took shape, it debated what powers the federal jurisdiction should have in the matter of industrial disputes and conciliation and arbitration. This would be a vexed question in the early decades of federation. Until the iconic *Engineers' Case* in 1920, dispute resolution would reflect a tendency to refer to American precedents and favour State jurisdictions. In the parliamentary debates over the Conciliation and Arbitration Bill on 25 August 1903, Glynn was clearly opposed to wide-scale legislation to allow any federal jurisdiction to override State powers in industrial disputation. However, he also spoke up for workers' rights and voluntary negotiation, while anticipating many of the dilemmas to come:

I contend that powers are sought which are a manifest extension of those granted under the Constitution. Apparently, the principle upon which the government are acting is to gather into an Act of Parliament all the powers they consider expedient, in order to carry out their policy, and leave it to the High Court to decide whether those powers are constitutional or otherwise. What a splendid opening that would afford the lawyers.[77]

As the decades have since shown, where conciliation and arbitration – and indeed most industrial matters – are concerned, it has been much to the advantage of the lawyers. Furthermore, in arguing for voluntary arbitration, Glynn might also have been arguing for a settlement of industrial disputes not dissimilar to the enterprise bargaining a century later. Quoting the British Iron Trade Commission on American industrial conditions, he backed the idea, saying:

> . . . we find in the report of the Commission evidence of the growing success of extensive voluntary arbitration . . . four of the leading trades – the stove builders, the founders, the machinists and the printing trades – have entered into formal agreements between employers and employees in regard to the voluntary settlement of disputes.[78]

On race, Glynn often stood against the tide, speaking out against any blanket denial of residence to individuals on account of ethnic background. In a case where a Chinese resident of Australia was prevented (under the Immigration Restriction Act) from being joined by his wife and children, Glynn spoke in the House on 7 September 1911, saying, "The Eastern races in India, China and Japan number something like 670,000,000 and I hope that the government, with a sense of statesmanship and fairness, will consider whether it is not possible . . . in accordance with the law which was in force up to 1905, that [alien] men before that year can have their wives here."[79]

As Sir Robert Garran recognised of his federation colleague, Glynn formed his views from careful reading and individual experience. He belonged to an age where political parties in Australia were barely at the threshold and groupings among politicians more likely to be formed around the strength of individual leaders or single issues. This fluidity in federal politics saw administrations come and go with uncertainty around where many individual MPs' support lay. Some of Glynn's attitudes could have found him safely inside Labor ranks – such as his comment on 25 August 1903 in the House that "some of the worst evils of the factory system were the result of the principle of lassez-faire". Yet, he was also a supporter of the market, telling the House on 5 October 1904 that, "I say it is the duty of the State to control monopoly, but not to interfere with the true sphere of private enterprise, not to obtrude upon the thousand and one other lines of our industrial activity."[80] In the same sitting, Glynn pronounced what for him was his fundamental perspective on his role as legislator:

> Considering the record of mistakes that legislators have made, we ought to keep the State to its true province, which is to destroy monopoly, to afford to all equal opportunity, and to leave to private enterprise, to individual intelligence and guidance, the task of perfecting and sustaining what is best in our industrial and social civilisation.

For Glynn, the way forward was by reason and debate, and respect for differing views, a far cry from today's noisy mob advocacy to be found in social media, 'fake' news and social disruption.

The River Murray and riparian rights

Glynn's belief in the steady accumulation of facts, an ability to argue a case and the recognition of the need to compromise where sensible as the mark of true leadership is best illustrated in the work he did for the River Murray Waters Agreement over nearly two decades.

In a series of articles for *The Advertiser*, beginning on 18 April 1898, Glynn had explained to South Australians what the new proposed Constitution for the federation of the Australian colonies entailed. Significantly, as he introduced his topic, Glynn chose to illustrate the benefits to South Australia of section 51 of the Constitution, which allows the parliament to regulate interstate and international trade and commerce. Glynn wrote:

> . . . the Parliament of the Commonwealth could legislate for, not only the maintenance, but the improvement, of the navigability of inter-State rivers, and could limit to any extent necessitated by the maintenance of rivers as channels of commerce between States, the State powers arising from the possession of the waters.[81]

The issue of what was then called riparian rights was dear to the hearts of the colonists of South Australia. Not only was water a scarce resource in Australia's driest colony, the Murray River from its intersection with the Darling River at Wentworth was integral to South Australia's transport infrastructure. Glynn's argument was a good hook, but also one he held strong feelings about. He would spend the next decade and a half working towards a federal agreement on water rights and navigability around the Murray.

At the federation conventions, delegates had haggled over the control of the major rivers in the Murray-Darling basin, where navigation could be adversely affected by use of water for irrigation. South Australia's delegate, John Hannah Gordon MLC, put it plainly during the Melbourne session on 21 January 1898:

> The Darling is a stream which for geographical purposes has that name given to it for a portion of its course, but it forms part of a great system of water-courses. If any honourable member were to launch himself in a canoe at the head of either the Darling, the Murrumbidgee, the Lachlan, or the Murray, where would he find himself at the end of his journey? In South Australia. . . . Rivers which take their rise in New South Wales, but which run for huge distances through other colonies, cannot be described by the residents of New South Wales as "our rivers", using the term in the sense of exclusive and sole possession.[82]

In the discussion which followed, Alfred Deakin from Victoria, who had a recognised knowledge of riparian issues, argued the matters at hand – from the competition between rail and river rates, the use of water for irrigation, and the ways of using locks and dams to improve water availability, to the ill feeling of New South Wales over losing out financially in any federal control over the Murray-Darling basin. It was Deakin's conclusion that New South Wales needed to make a compromise for the sake of the whole nation:

> I feel that because New South Wales is the only colony that is asked to make a sacrifice in this matter, and is not yet prepared to make it, they should not shut the door on all future federal control of this great arterial system of

Australia. It would be an immense gain to the continent as a whole if the river system could be federalised, if the federalising of it could be effected without imperilling the interests of New South Wales.[83]

Shortly after Deakin had spoken, Glynn rose to push the case for federal control of the rivers. He concurred with the arguments put by Gordon and Deakin. He then went on to argue that, economically, as had been shown in the United Kingdom, transport by canals and rivers was much cheaper than rail and was returning as a favoured means of transport in many parts of the world. Co-operation over the river system between the States could only improve the prosperity of Australia.

On the negative side, Glynn described the various plans for dams and storage of river waters upstream in New South Wales and Victoria along the Darling and Murray rivers as seriously damaging to the navigability of the Murray River in South Australia, as well as harming the prospects of sheep farmers dependent on the waters of Lake Alexandria and Lake Albert which were already prone to become brackish when river levels were low. As he put it, "The upshot of the matter is that we must have federal action, or we cannot maintain existing rights in regard to the waters of those lakes in South Australia."[84] In another age, Glynn would have pointed to the environmental damage as well.

But Glynn was not finished. He went back into earlier discussions between New South Wales, Victoria, and South Australia over river usage and ways to deal with the competing interests. South Australia had requested a conference on river usage between the three colonies in 1857 but had been ignored. In 1863, a conference held in Melbourne passed a resolution upholding the benefit to "commerce, population and wealth" of a well-maintained and navigable Murray-Darling basin. In 1887, the Water Supply Commissions of Victoria and New South Wales had concluded they should "divide between them the whole of the waters of the Murray, from its source to the eastern boundary of South Australia". Challenged by New South Wales's William Lyne, that this was not true, Glynn produced evidence to the contrary, saying:

> I challenge the honorable member; they did arrive at that conclusion. There was a preliminary report or proposal in 1887, and South Australia remonstrated against the tenor of that report through Sir John Downer, who will be able to bear out my remarks. The minutes of that remonstrance and the terms of the report may be found in the Blue-books, which are to be seen in the Library.[85]

Lyne was out of his depth

Answering Lyne's objection, and a further query by Sir George Turner, Glynn was able to demonstrate the purpose of the commissions was eventually to arrive at "some common basis of federal action". In other words, there were compelling precedents for the federation delegates to reconsider the problem and come up with a workable solution. The obstacle to any proper outcome from these two colonial commissions had been Sir Henry Parkes, who had dissolved the New South Wales commission. "In every instance," said Glynn, "New South Wales endeavoured to frustrate joint action."[86] To which George Reid countered, "In other words, we have been slow to permit your interference with something that belongs to us." The hackles were well and truly raised. Barbs came quickly back and forth:

HIGGINS   Do the rain clouds belong to New South Wales?

SYMON   That is what it comes to.

KINGSTON And the heavens above.

REID   Victoria would stick to the Yarra till her last gasp.

It was a lively discussion. And made rather testy between Reid and Glynn as Reid claimed emphatically that the River Murray up to the South Australian border belonged exclusively to New South Wales. Glynn refuted the claim, at one moment saying to Reid, "I do not think the honourable member can show me a single statement in the *Constitution Act* or in the amending Act which gives more than the water-course to New South Wales."[87] Glynn maintained his unflappable calm by staying with references to precedents and treaties while Reid fell back on bluster, at one stage retorting, ". . . the question is settled, because we are stronger than you are," after Glynn had remarked that "there is no such thing as [international] law existing, except the right of the strongest". Glynn then took delegates through an historical review of "international comity" over a hundred years. He pointed out that, "The right of empire over any of the great arterial rivers of Europe has thus ceased to confer any exclusive privilege of navigation upon the nation which enjoys that right."[88]

Yet, it was soon back to the fundamentals with a long series of responses from New South Wales's Joseph Carruthers:

> Nothing that has been done in New South Wales in regard to the use of the water of the Darling has interfered with navigation. On the contrary, we have spent thousands and tens of thousands of pounds in rendering that river navigable, not for the benefit of the Government and the people of New South Wales, but largely for the benefit of

the Government and the people of South Australia who derive all the profits from the water carriage to their ports.

Glynn had been arguing the case for South Australia's water rights for over a decade and had been a member of the South Australian royal commission on the Murray waters in 1887. But the environmental conditions in Australia in the leadup to Federation impacted severely on all eastern States. A prolonged drought hit the continent after years of economic depression. Don Garden has described in "The Federation Drought of 1895-1903, El Niño and Society in Australia" how Australians faced hard and dangerous times:

> During the 1896 heatwave, furnace like winds from central Australia pushed temperatures well into the forties Celsius across much of the eastern half of the continent, setting new records and causing great suffering from heat and diseases, and numerous deaths. Conditions were particularly bad in outback New South Wales where there were reports of heat up to 52°C. The town of Bourke had an average over three weeks of 44°C, including four consecutive days of 48°C. Those who could had fled Bourke by train, but some 160 people died of heat and disease. The summer of 1897-98 was even hotter and windier in parts of eastern Australia. Many towns ran short of water and there were more deaths from heat and outbreaks of typhoid.[89]

As a new federal government was being proposed and debated, with uncertainty as to its success, climate disaster and economic conditions made discussion of water rights too much of a hard basket. Even the River Murray had dried in places to make it impossible to navigate. But with the formation of a central government – as Glynn recognised immediately – a solution needed to be found, however long it took. In 1902, an interstate royal commission was set up to tackle the Murray basin water rights issue, authorised by the prime minister and the premiers of New South Wales, South Australia, and Victoria. Glynn put the case for South Australia. While the devastating drought pressed the issue of water needs for irrigation in New South Wales and Victoria, it equally pushed as critical the issue of navigation and water rights further downstream in South Australia.

With Federation, regular premiers' conferences made collaboration a feature of State and federal arrangements. Speaking during the Address-in-Reply to the Governor-General's speech on 27 May 1903, Glynn tackled the issue of protection but soon moved to the question of water rights and the Murray, saying, "There is no doubt that the relative rights of the riparian States in the rivers, and the best use and just apportionment of the waters, is one of the biggest questions that Australian statesmanship can face."

In many respects, Glynn was the stone in the shoe for New South Wales and Victoria in the question of the Murray River. Like a dog unwilling to give up its bone, Glynn argued and stayed on the case. Debate dragged on for another year with Glynn arguing in the House on 28 July 1904 that the proposed Burrinjuck Dam on the Murrumbidgee would dam "one and a half times the quantity contained in Sydney Harbour" and going on to explain that:

> My objection to these schemes is that they are all haphazard and disconnected without any regard to Inter-State co-relation of riparian rights, or the federal sphere. No consideration is given to the quality of water, in fact, and in law, available to meet them, or to the conditions under which alone irrigation can be made to pay. I hold that it is

our duty, as Federal representatives, having regard to the reasonable necessities of all the States, and to the interests of the Commonwealth, as guardian of the Inter-State waterways, to ascertain what are really the possibilities of economical irrigation and Inter-State navigation.[90]

Glynn was ahead of his time in this matter. It would still be some years before any agreement was reached.

South Australia had nothing to lose by pressing on. Asked by South Australia's Attorney-General, Robert Homberg, in February 1905, to prepare a brief on the rights of States to the water of the Murray and its tributaries, Glynn produced a 150,000-word document, subsequently reviewed by two KCs – Josiah Symon and Isaac Isaacs – who supported the case Glynn had made in the document.[91] At the premiers' conference in April 1906, the premier of South Australia, Thomas Price, used Glynn's document to argue the South Australian case. The arguments had force and a committee was set up to draft a bill to give effect to plans to compensate South Australia for its loss of water from schemes higher up on the Murray. Glynn became South Australia's representative on that committee.

As Glynn's diary entries for 1907 show, negotiations were drawn out. At the May 1907 premiers' conference in Brisbane, Glynn could only manage a meeting with New South Wales premier, Joseph Carruthers, while at the Queensland Turf Club. Further discussions followed back in Sydney and, after hours of discussion, an agreement was reached with Glynn telling the South Australian premier, Tom Price, that the negotiations were delicate and there was a need not to damn the agreement with "faint praise". It was not all South Australia would have liked, but it was better than what had been decided a year before.

It would not be until 1914 that a satisfactory agreement on the shared uses of the waters of the Murray-Darling basin was reached. By then, Glynn was the Minister for External Affairs in the Ministry of Joseph Cook. As such, Glynn had influence and had been able to secure Cook's support for a considerable Commonwealth financial contribution to locks and weirs on the Murray. This spearheaded agreement from the three States involved to contribute equally under a River Murray Commission. On 9 September 1914, just days before the Cook Ministry would lose office to Andrew Fisher's Labor Party, the agreement was signed. In 1915, this agreement would become the Commonwealth's River Murray Waters Act.

Over many years, Glynn played a crucial role in the outcome of the River Murray Waters Act as acknowledged by New South Wales premier, William Holman, at the laying of the foundation stone for the William R Randall Lock at Blanchetown in early June 1915. Holman spoke of Glynn's "political engineering" as being of more importance to the scheme than that of the eminent engineers who had constructed the lock. Glynn, said Holman, was "very difficult to get around in any way" and in this he was guided by two principles – "one the Federal spirit and the other State rights". Holman praised Glynn for "paving the way for a friendly settlement of the outstanding difficulties".[92] What Holman recognised was Glynn's combination of tenacity and ability to use reason to overcome obstacles. A trait that had seen Glynn not only survive, but emerge as a prominent figure in his life in Australia. In July 1913, the South Australian government recommended Glynn's appointment as King's Counsel for his work on the River Murray Agreement.

Ireland and the Crown

On 22 July 1910, Glynn was complimented by *The Argus* (not known for its tolerant views on Catholics) for his speech during the debate the previous day over the parliamentary motion moved by an Irish-born and Catholic Labor MP, Hugh Mahon, to remove from the British Coronation Oath all words objectionable or offensive to Catholics.[93] In his speech, Glynn exhibited a leadership that could bridge a divide by avoiding the temptation for sectarian bitterness. Mahon's motion also began carefully by pointing out that "since full freedom of religious belief obtains throughout the Empire, the British Sovereign should not be called on to make any Declaration offensive to the religious convictions of any section of Your Majesty's subjects". There was only one religion, however, where offence was given in the Coronation Oath – that was towards the Catholic Church's doctrine of transubstantiation (real presence of Christ in the Eucharist) and its reverence for the Virgin Mary. These beliefs were referred to in the Oath as "superstitious and idolatrous".

Taking an objective approach, Glynn argued the offensive words were "framed at a time when men had not yet learned the real elements of religious toleration". He could empathise—again in hindsight – adding that it was thought "the Protestant succession was in danger". However, he added, that "spirit of intolerance [was] displayed by mistaken zealots of every creed, [and] is not the spirit of our days".

For all that, Glynn did not let his generous empathy be the last word and later drew his audience's attention to their history of intertwined faiths, "We must also remember . . . that the religious faith that is subject to obloquy under a misapprehension or perversion of its real significance was the faith of England for nearly a thousand years. The faith of the founder of that Abbey in which the Kings and Queens of England, Catholic and Protestant alike, are buried – that Imperial mausoleum in which so many tombs and epitaphs speak of the illustrious dead, once of different creeds but now of common certitude, who made England what it is . . ."[94]

From his early days in Australia and his failed 1881 publication, *Irish State Trials,* Glynn had thrown his support publicly and vocally behind the cause of Home Rule for Ireland. In his *Kapunda Herald* editorials and in his membership of the colonial Irish land leagues, Glynn had argued that Britain should agree to allow the Irish self-rule over their domestic politics – much like the Scots and Welsh enjoy in the United Kingdom today with devolution. Speaking in the House of Representatives during the Home Rule for Ireland debate on 17 May 1905, Glynn argued, ". . . whether we believe, or do not believe, in the principle of Home Rule, those of us who are sincere are actuated by the common motive of desire to promote the integrity and welfare of the Empire, as well as the prosperity of each of its merits. . . . Under either an autocratic or a democratic Government, autonomy is the only alternative to centralisation. . . . It is in a restricted federalism that the solution of the Irish question may be found."[95] Glynn would become a supporter of Westminster MP John Redmond's Irish nationalist cause, which helped push through the Irish Home Rule Act in September 1914.

Events in Ireland, however, took their own course. With the outbreak of World War I, Home Rule was interrupted. A festering of unrest continued around Irish republican groups of radicals and culminated in the Easter Rising of 1916. The small cluster of Irish rebels that turned Dublin into a week's bloodbath was hot-headed, divided and certainly wild in the planning or lack of it. With the Irish Republican Brotherhood's acquiescence, Roger Casement had attempted to smuggle arms into Ireland from Germany. The rebels were dealing with Britain's enemy in their own struggle against the United Kingdom.

Unsurprisingly, the Easter Rising was anathema to Paddy Glynn on the other side of the globe. As the war began in 1914, Glynn's patriotism was marked and evident in speeches he gave, described in Gerald O'Collins's biography as "a eulogy to Empire".[96] As the news of the Dublin uprising came through, Glynn voiced the feelings of many a good Redmondite, telling *The Advertiser* on 1 May 1916:

> I think that the unfortunate trouble amongst a section of the irreconcilables in Ireland may be traced to propagandists in America and Germany. . . . It affects only a very small percentage of the population and so far as it is militant it may be said to have existed only within the last two or three years. . . . Sir Roger Casement's attack was chiefly on Mr Redmond and the Nationalists. . . . As a matter of fact Sir Roger Casement is not, and never was, a prominent Irish Nationalist.

In his interview with *The Advertiser*, Glynn was at pains to talk up the important role many Irishmen were playing in fighting alongside Imperial troops: "The enemy has learned on more than one stricken field in France how Irishmen can fight. . . . These were men that represent, I believe, the Irish people, and whose loyalty and spirit never wavered at a critical moment of our history." A few days later, Glynn's diary entry for 4 May 1916 refers to speaking at a Murray Bridge recruiting meeting and that he was leaving for Vancouver on 11 May. Glynn had been selected as one of ten Australian parliamentarians to join a delegation to inspect the war administration. The delegation was at the invitation of the Empire Parliamentary Association and included ten Canadians, six South Africans, four New Zealanders and two from Newfoundland. So Glynn was preparing for five months' travel abroad, accompanied by Abigail, to the United States, Britain, and Europe.

Under pressure of a very busy official schedule, Glynn attended packed meetings in Britain and made a visit to Paris and Australian troops on the Western Front. On 4 August 1916, writing to his mother in Ireland after seeing the war at close quarters, Glynn reflected on his experience of the war:

> I was right in the firing lines . . . The Australians had a fearful job where I was, near Armentieres. I saw several of the boys coming in wounded after their great push, but the bulk of the Australians were in Poziere. I know, having visited the wounded at London hospitals on Sunday, that in many cases only a few out of hundreds were left. One Battalion in which was one of my clerks – practically a private secretary – seems to be completely wiped out, but the spirit of the boys is unbroken. Hoping to see you next week.[97]

Glynn, as he promised his mother, had managed to squeeze in a visit to Ireland before leaving the UK. It was a decades long, and much waited for, reunion with his 81-year-old mother and those of his siblings and friends still living there. But the trip to Britain and the Front would only strengthen Glynn's support for Australia's commitment to the war effort.

On their return to Australia, on 20 October 1916, the Glynns came ashore to the rancour and bitterness of the debates during the first conscription plebiscite called by Labor prime minister Billy Hughes to solve the recruitment crisis. Hughes's support for conscription had sharply divided his party and, with the loss of the plebiscite, Labor removed Hughes as leader on 24 November, leaving him to walk out of the party room with a contingent of 24 Labor MPs who supported him. Cook's Liberals were then the largest party in the House and eventually came to an agreement with Hughes over a coalition. Glynn's diary entry for 11 February 1917, records that he had been against a coalition with Hughes's Labor team but his motion in the party room had been lost and he was then appointed by the Liberal members to go with Cook and Forrest to thrash out a deal with the Hughes MPs. His diary entry for 13 February records that agreement had been reached about most matters necessary to form a coalition: "Today the basis, with some heads of policy, were settled. One point only still remains; the question of a change in the head of the Defence Department."

The new ministry under Hughes as prime minister took office on 17 February 1917, with Glynn appointed Minister for Home and Territories in the new Nationalist government, the only Catholic and the only South Australian in the cabinet. That Glynn stood out in such an isolated way in the Hughes cabinet says much about Glynn, the Hughes government and the times. McMahon Glynn, with his independence of thought and his Irish Catholic background was then an unlikely non-Labor figure in the Commonwealth parliament. But he had come to his position largely from his support for free trade and his views on economics, which left him on the non-Labor side of the parliament, holding a mixture of liberal and independently conservative views. With the exit of Billy Hughes and his supporters from Labor over conscription and their coalition with Joseph Cook's conservatives, Glynn would become part of what was to become one of Australia's most reactionary governments. And his trust in a possible non-sectarian faith in civil society under the Crown would soon be under considerable challenge.

A last stand – the case of Father Charles Jerger

Writing to the superior of the Catholic Church's Passionist order of priests in Sydney's Marrickville on 25 October 1916, Hugh Mahon – who had not followed Hughes out of the Labor Party – gave what he believed to be a fair opinion on the case of Passionist priest Father Charles Jerger, who had been accused of seditious remarks in one of his Sunday sermons:

> I left Melbourne on Friday. . . . Up to the time I left [the Hughes Ministry] no complaint regarding Father Charles' remarks had reached the Defence Department. I shall not be surprised to hear that the incident has blown over; it seems a very trifling thing at the worst, and only a very excitable imagination in these exciting times could have magnified it so as to call for official enquiry. I think the good father should go on with his useful and beneficent work as if the incident had never occurred . . .[98]

This was a telling reflection on what should have always have been regarded exactly as Mahon described – "a very trifling thing at the worst". However, it was also a mistaken judgement on what would eventually become one of Australia's more shameful acts of intolerance, bigotry, and injustice. After years of incarceration, Father Charles Jerger would be deported from Australia on 26 July 1920, amid cries of protest – not only from Catholics. His crime? According to the witness of one female parishioner at his church in the Sydney suburb of Marrickville (whose testimony was claimed as inaccurate by other attendees on the day), Charles Jerger was supposed to have said in a sermon on 24 September 1916, shortly before the first plebiscite on conscription, that he was not going to talk about the war but "Why should 3 out of our best men out of every 50 of the population be taken away? What had England done?"

Mrs McCall, who claimed this was what the priest had said, made an official statement to the police after extracting a promise that she would not be involved in any official enquiry. Her testimony would be refuted by the priest and others who heard the sermon. But, in the hysteria of the times, Charles Jerger, who had not been legally naturalised as a British subject, was eventually interned as an alien in early 1918. In spite of having lived in Britain and Australia since 1874, he was eventually deported from what had been his homeland since he was five years old. The full details of the campaign to have Jerger condemned can be read in Gerard Henderson's "The Deportation of Charles Jerger" in *Labour History*.[99] Father Jerger died just six years later in 1927, at the age of fifty-eight.

As Henderson makes clear, Jerger's real crime was to have been German-born and to have dared to comment on the war at all. From the outbreak of war in late 1914, Australians of German heritage – even some with three generations living in Australia – were alienated and many thousands were incarcerated. Then, with the heightened tensions of the bitter conscription debates from late 1916, many came to regard opposition to conscription as opposition to the war and a mark of disloyalty to Britain and Australia. Tasmanian Labor MP and opponent of conscription, Joseph Lyons, later Tasmanian premier and prime minister, was all but thrown off a bridge during the conscription debates.

Jerger, however, held a double impediment. From the time of the Easter Rising in Dublin, in April 1916, Australian Catholics had become suspect as potential traitors with their loyalty to Rome rather than the Church of England and their overwhelmingly Irish heritage. In the heightened and excitable tenor of public discussion, even mild objections to the war effort could be seen by loyalists as seditious. In the case of Jerger, it was Alderman John Thomas Ness of Marrickville who led the campaign to have the government intern and deport the priest. Ness was a loyalist Protestant. On Sunday, 10 March 1918, at a meeting of the local branch of the Australian League of Loyalty in the St Peters Town Hall, Sydney, the Reverend J. A. Waddell spoke of being a Protestant warrior for half a century and that Dr Mannix and his class wanted to keep Ireland "in turmoil in order to give the Vatican greater temporal power". This was pure smear aimed at what many extremist Protestants of the day continued to see as the tentacles of an ancient order in Vatican City. At the same meeting, Ness stated he was "jealous of Empire and country" and "found he was forced to throw tolerance to the wind, take off the gloves, and fight the Roman Catholic Church".[100]

In this atmosphere, as a minister in the Hughes government, for Paddy Glynn to take up the case of Father Charles Jerger was courageous. But he did. Gerard Henderson is critical of Glynn's lack of passion for the cause, but Glynn's letters to the Minister for Defence, George Pearce, and to Jerger's superiors, show that Glynn worked hard to intervene as best he could. As the sole Catholic in the ministry, until Senator Edward Russell joined the cabinet on 27 March 1918, Glynn walked the Catholic-

Protestant divide as never before. His support for the war and conscription was unquestioned. But his sense of the injustice in the case roused his feelings.

Always a rational and tolerant voice, Glynn's best efforts failed to win any change of hardened feeling in what had become a strongly Protestant 'King-and-country' government. At the time of Mrs McCall's accusation against Father Jerger, the Hughes Labor government had yet to splinter – which it did following the 1916 conscription plebiscite. The Labor MPs who followed Hughes out of the Labor Party were less likely to have many Catholics among them. The Cook-Hughes coalition that followed was strongly supported by anti-Catholic sectarians, by then convinced they stood against the forces of Rome – especially since the Easter Rising in Dublin.

By 15 February 1918, when Jerger was eventually interned, the political atmosphere had very much changed. Germany was looking more and more as if it might defeat the allies, and the Hughes ministry had become hardened against Jerger. A small contingent of accusers had by now joined Mrs McCall in condemning Jerger as some sort of single-handed German fifth column. Absurd as the evidence proved this to be, hysteria had whipped up around Jerger, largely behind the leadership of Alderman Ness.

Shortly after Jerger's internment, Glynn wrote to his colleague and Minister for Defence, George Pearce, appealing to him to reconsider Jerger's internment. He communicated with Jerger's Passionist order's superiors, based in the Sydney suburb of Marrickville, and Archbishop Michael Kelly of Sydney. On 26 March, Glynn wrote again that he had received "further information" which backed up the statements he had received from Father Ryan, head of the order. On the basis of this evidence, Glynn argued that "the internment of Father Jerger was a mistake", and told Pearce:

> In the opinion of those who know him intimately, and . . . have some moral or disciplinary relation to his conduct as a Passionist and member of the community, he is a man of high character and unimpeachable loyalty. The spirit, if not the written rules, of orders of the Catholic Church make, and on the whole secure, loyalty to the state as one of the obligations of members. Father Jerger acted consistently with the duty thus imposed upon him.[101]

Pearce's reply was not reassuring and attempted to twist Glynn's words to suggest he was asserting facts of which he had no knowledge. Pearce also made no bones about his view that Jerger had no claim to being British as he had registered himself as alien and been born in Germany in 1869. "Father Jerger," wrote Pearce, "is therefore an enemy (German) subject." Furthermore, Pearce regarded it as irrelevant that Jerger's father had been naturalised as an Australian in 1907 and that there had been no evidence supplied that Jerger's father was naturalised in England at an earlier date.

Pearce's letter makes clear that he had already decided the case – he saw no possibility that the accusers could be lying or simply exaggerating because they might be hysterically opposed to Jerger as a German. Or that the gossip and a political campaign had taken a slight incident well beyond the facts. Pearce continued:

> His [Jerger's] use of words, disloyal and contrary to the public safety, have been proved to the satisfaction of the Minister, as required by the War Precautions Act and

Regulations even for a naturalised enemy subject. Even naturalised Germans have been interned on evidence not nearly so strong as in this case. His position as a Minister of religion cannot affect the question.[102]

Glynn replied to Pearce on 12 April, rebutting Pearce's interpretation of Glynn's 24 March letter and standing firm, ending with, "I submitted to you considerations presented to me with a view to their being considered in relation to the evidence or grounds of suspicion, whatever they are, on which the internment has been directed. You doubtless have given, or will give them, full consideration."[103] Pearce's reply on 24 April, began sarcastically by noting Glynn's "niceties of legal distinctions" which, Pearce added, was not something he was trained in. He then went on to dismiss Glynn's appeals and assert that "all German subjects are liable to internment without any cause shown, and Father Jerger is a subject of the German Emperor".[104]

For all that, Glynn stayed on the case. In June, he wrote to Pearce asking for consideration to be given to Jerger's deprived living conditions at his place of internment. He was constantly followed by a guard. Glynn asked if that was necessary. Jerger had also been refused a request from the Passionist superior at Marrickville that, in consideration of Jerger's frail health, they could build a weatherboard room for him rather than have him continue to live in the camp's tent accommodation. Glynn closed by mentioning that he had spoken to Pearce separately about "the question of Father Jerger's internment generally". By August, Glynn was writing about the treatment of Jerger in the camp as being made excessively difficult by the apparent intervention of certain guards who were "constantly blocking and thwarting the good intention of the higher authorities", and who ensured that Jerger was continually searched at the camp and that his food was extremely poor.

For many in contemporary Australia, what Glynn was trying to do was intervene in the case of a detained non-citizen. The case was made more difficult with the clamour of the political campaign against Jerger in particular. Glynn persisted in arguing the known facts; the government persisted in carrying out what it saw as a politically justified decision. It is a similar scenario in contemporary times in the many cases of detained refugees who have arrived unlawfully in Australia – except, in the midst of the hysteria over Germans and the war, the Jerger case was more about political scapegoating. Jerger had resided lawfully and for most of his life in Britain or a British colony. Added to that, evidence that he had been wrongfully detained was shamefully and deliberately ignored.

During 1919, there were a few glimmers of hope. Glynn was able to write to Father Henry at Marrickville on 11 September 1918 that the Defence Minister had responded to the many complaints with an answer that indicated Jerger's conditions would improve as the Ministry had approved "interned Clergymen being accorded treatment as officers".[105] On 21 February 1919, Glynn wrote to the Reverend Peter O'Reilly of Woollahra, Sydney that his "correspondence with the Defence Department, apart from oral communications with the Minister, has extended over 12 months". Glynn was still hopeful, adding:

> The fact is I have pressed the matter upon those who control
> his internment time after time, and am endeavouring to get
> his case disposed of now without a reference to a Board of
> Enquiry. It would have been well, in my opinion, if such

reference had taken place twelve months ago. I can repeat my assurance that if Father Jerger is released on a verbal undertaking by a member of his Order as to anything reasonable required, no harm will ensue.[106]

On 11 March, Glynn wrote to Archbishop Kelly of Sydney that, "I am hopeful of a report favourable to his release being obtained". He was even more hopeful that a way through would be found. In a letter to Father Callistus Henry on 3 July, Glynn advised that he had brought Jerger's case up in cabinet meetings over two days and that he had told the minister "the proper course would be to release Father Jerger at once without further enquiry". He added that the minister had spoken to the Board regarding Jerger's case, "asking to expedite it", and he had assured Glynn that, as promised, Jerger would "have a full opportunity of giving evidence himself or, should he desire it, you or anyone else to speak on his behalf and state the facts as they really are".[107]

Glynn's letters to Father Henry and Jerger's sister Mrs Ward continued over some months. In spite of Glynn's confidence Jerger would be released, from advice he received at the ministerial level, Jerger's case continued to be frustrated at the departmental level and at the detention centre. This is a familiar occurrence a century later, where officials along the chain of command often act in accordance with their own prejudices and believe they are authorised to make executive decisions. Nothing improved in relation to Jerger's release and Jerger was even prevented from visiting his dying mother. Instead, he was allowed out for a day to attend her funeral in September. Glynn continued to request intervention for Jerger until the federal election of 1919, in December, took his attention. In spite of a strong German representation among the voters of Angus, Glynn lost his seat. His actions for Jerger had not been public and he represented a government hard-edged about Germanic Australians.

With Glynn gone from the ministry, Jerger's case lingered on. Without a champion at ministerial level, officials applied the letter of the law. The Solicitor-General, Sir Robert Garran, offered his advice on 29 March 1920 that he was convinced that Jerger was "an active propagandist against the cause of the Allies" during the war.[108] Glynn was kept up to date with the Jerger case by his supporters and made further representations, to no avail. On 5 May 1920, Glynn wrote to the Reverend Callistus Henry that he had heard from a contact in the government that "the intention is to deport" and that "they are simply waiting for an opportunity".[109] In spite of this, Glynn continued to stretch his contacts for intervention – even writing to the prime minister.

Many groups sought the release of Father Jerger. The protests had become widespread by July 1920, with many non-Catholics joining the uproar. Maritime unionists refused to work on the first ship chosen to deport Jerger. But the government stood firm and Jerger was eventually deported from Fremantle on a ship with a 'coolie' crew. Efforts to have Jerger exonerated continued nonetheless. *The Southern Cross* Catholic newspaper reported on 13 August 1920 that Glynn had handed to Jerger's counsel a "copy of a full statement of the case" which had been taken to Melbourne and which demonstrated "that there was no evidence against Father Jerger and that it was difficult even to ascertain the charges". The paper reported that Glynn was in "the best position to give an opinion, and his opinion [was] that no proof of any disloyalty was ever brought forward".[110]

With the deportation of Father Jerger and the subsequent failure to exonerate him, Glynn's trust in reason and argument and the facts had taken a beating. And Archbishop Daniel Mannix's public statement in March 1918 that a government had interned a priest when they could not intern an archbishop (himself) had resulted in the tragic consequences that Mannix had envisaged.

Glynn's legacy for a nation

In an article entitled "The End of the Century", written for *The Southern Cross* as the nineteenth century closed, Glynn opined, "Everything is transient and in flux; welcome succeeds farewell; God, the unconditioned, alone remains, Whose unity, as St Augustine says, is the mould of all things."[111] As Alan Atkinson has commented in his study of Glynn's convention speeches, Glynn's God was "'the Unseen' . . . hardly solid enough even to be 'he'".[112] He had formed his notions of civil society and its spiritual underpinnings over decades of reading of the classics. The copious notebooks he kept, now in the National Library in Canberra, record his thoughts as he prepared for speeches and arguments. Sir Robert Garran, in his political memoir, *Prosper the Commonwealth*, refers to Glynn as having "a prodigious memory" and that he could declaim, for hours on end, pages of Burke, or whole plays of Shakespeare. But Garran added that, although a fine speaker, "I do not think he ever relied on the inspiration of the moment; his orations showed signs of careful preparation".[113] This reference from Garran smacks of faint praise. Too often in politics, it is the theatrical appeal of the demagogue which catches the imagination, more than the rigorous argument of those who come well prepared.

In today's world, driven by information overload and opinion as news, careful preparation could never be a weakness. Yet more emotive and polemical performers do catch the attention in hard-edged debate. Glynn caught the attention of journalists who recognised his erudition and style as a public speaker, although too often his serious and scholarly words could take parliamentary colleagues into knowledgeable diversions not fully appreciated in the cut-and-thrust of division. Deakin, commenting on Glynn, put it more astutely than Garran: "Glynn, with greater assiduity of research, splendid and carefully polished diction and stiff delivery, never caught or kept the ear of an Assembly, like all popular bodies jealous and antagonistic to scholarship and style, unless forced upon them by more practical merits."[114]

Glynn's parliamentary and convention speeches were laced with research, comparative studies, legal precedents, and statistics. At times, too, he would divert to the thought of some literary or political hero. His references (largely to men) go back through the ages and are so widely sprayed as to offer a snapshot bibliography in any study of Western civilisation. They last as documents of timeless argument, backed by the study and gravitas of earlier scholars and statesmen. Imagine a federal parliament today where a speaker hard at argument over water conservation suddenly moved to recite thirteen lines of Shakespeare's *Troilus and Cressida* as Glynn did in a speech in the House of Representatives on 28 July 1904. Or a rejoinder to Isaac Isaacs during the convention sitting on 9 February 1898 in Melbourne, after Isaacs had quoted an opinion from a contemporary political theorist regarding deadlocks in the Senate, when Glynn responded, "Another theorist, Bagehot, said the same thing forty years ago." Glynn communicated, more eloquently than others, the underpinnings and traditions of the Westminster system and Western civilisation, a system and a civilisation which had brought the continent of Australia into the global community. A system and a civilisation that Glynn firmly believed was the strength of its existence.

That Deakin felt Glynn could lose a parliamentary audience from colleagues' resentment of his scholarship is a telling reminder of the raw and pragmatic nature of Australian politics, in which personality rather than scholarly authority captures voters. Paul Hasluck, in another time, might well illustrate some of Glynn's style as a public figure. Deakin was accurate in his estimation of Glynn's overall political ambience, but his evaluation also suggests a limited intellectual depth in the argument and debate to be found in Australia's parliamentary environment. Glynn was a free thinker in many respects, chiselling his ideas from the experiences and theories of notable thinkers and statesmen who had gone before him. At the Australasian Federation Conference on 24 March 1897, he spoke at length on his views of a coming constitutional federation of the colonies, previewing debates to come a century later:

> On the whole, the general teaching of history is to show that, though a monarchical Federation is by no means theoretically impossible, yet a republican Federation is far more likely to exist as a permanent and flourishing system. We may, therefore, in the general course of comparison, practically assume that a Federal State will also be a republican State. Of course, that will not tell against our Federation, because we really set up a crowned republic.[115]

In an essay entitled *Imperial Union* and published as a pamphlet, written around 1918-19, Glynn argued that the dominions should retain their independence and that any sort of Imperial federation would not work:

> Imperial strength through central and dominion self-government, is both end and means. The freer within reason, the less subject to internal problems and consequent dissensions, the relations and parts of the Empire are, the greater must be our strength, material and moral, in international affairs. . . . Race, distance, traditions, and local points of view, must tell against the comparative efficacy of the federal form of tie.[116]

For all his erudition on show, Glynn was a well-loved and attractive individual. Cartoonists and journalists found him to have a colourful character for portraiture. He saw beyond the immediate in ways that, only a century later, have resonance. Yet, he could also plough on, as in the River Murray Waters Agreement, to extract practical outcomes from conciliation and compromise. In the political times of Patrick McMahon Glynn, bigotry and prejudice abounded as it does in our own today. It was Glynn's way, however, not to revolt or agitate against his opponents. He preferred to remain strong in the face of debate, while seeking wherever possible to meet halfway, or at least strive for reasoned understanding. In this, Glynn has many messages for contemporary life.

Christian Bergmann has written that a study of Glynn's convention speeches reveals him as "a man on the fringes, intellectually speaking, since he displayed concerns that nobody else was willing to attest to or agree with".[117] But those concerns, a century and more later, continue to echo: the Murray-Darling basin; the need to find ways to a more equitable distribution and collection of tax; how to answer bigotry and mob pressure in the social fabric; the vexed question of section 116 of the Constitution and freedom of religion; and an eternal question – whether increasing secularisation and materialism should – or can – hold a nation together.

In any debate about Australia's future or identity, Patrick McMahon Glynn – his life, his inspiration, his intellectual heroes, and his ideas – deserves resurrecting for scholarly consideration.

Responding to Anne Henderson

1. The biographer's tracks

Patrick Mullins

Biography has always had the whiff of illegitimacy about it. To a subject, it often feels a form of theft or assassination. To a subject's family, it is voyeuristic and profane. To the philosopher, its purported recreation of the past and relation of what is in the subject's mind is a dishonest strain for the impossible.[1] To the historian, it is suspect for its elevation of the individual and its understatement of vast, impersonal, and unconscious forces. To the sceptic, it elevates and whitewashes. To the critic, it stretches and distorts a life to fit an instructional or propagandist frame. To the artist, no less, it is an exercise in drudgery: "The biographer is bound," Virginia Woolf once intoned.[2] Around political biography these criticisms come much stronger, to the point that the whole genre appears so resolutely suspect and old-fashioned that its practitioners may, as the late Geoffrey Bolton once remarked, be compared to the craftsman who, in an age of Swatch factories, persists in making by time honoured method the antique cuckoo clock.[3]

And yet political biography continues to flourish. The genre attracts a stream of craftsmen, as Bolton's example – in his lives of Forrest, Boyer, Wollaston, Barton, and Hasluck – attests. It remains a popular genre, as the front table of any bookshop shows; and the critical space afforded to political biography within the mainstream press and (increasingly) the academy is considerable.

The foremost reason for this is the dual opportunity that political biography offers. In making the individual life intelligible – the basic aim of any biography – writer and reader give attention to the individual *and* the context of that individual's life. The first focus, on the individual (to the point that some call biography a cousin to the novel), offers opportunity for both the 'moral improvement' that Plutarch would commend and the understanding, knowledge, and judgment that the historian, philosopher, sceptic, or even interested citizen might desire. Simultaneously, that focus on the individual offers both to writer and reader a path, a thread, a way to make sense of the historical context of the life at hand. The narrative form that is the invariable backbone of a biography is especially conducive to this. Though guarding against the 'bad King John heresy',[*] the rigorous and well-told biography facilitates an understanding of the individual, the past, and the individual's role within it.[4] Inhabiting a space between history and literature, biography draws on both: it builds from the historical record, evaluating and showing character, to tell a story. Second, the diligently researched and well-written biography, as Henry James's biographer, Leon Edel, once wrote, "reveals the individual within history, within an ethos and a social complex".[5] While the spotlight remains fixed on the individual, its sweep takes in more. A good biography will illuminate place, culture, society, institutions, and processes, contextualising the life as it has been lived, drawing events together as they have been experienced. The individual life thereby becomes a way to understand much more than the individual life.

---

[*] The belief that what is of decisive import in history, to the exclusion of other factors, is the character and behaviour of individuals.

To do this calls for a myriad of skills and talents. Biographers should at once be genealogists, psychiatrists, social scientists, journalists, portrait painters, historians, scholars, judges, story-tellers, resourceful and persistent pursuers of the truth – whatever they deem that to be. "More than the specialist historian," the late British political scientist Ben Pimlott tells us, "the biographer needs to be a jack-of-all-trades". Yet this must come with the necessary caveat: "Hence [he or she] is liable to be considered a master of none."[6] There are, moreover, explanations that a political biographer must offer: how the subject fits into their culture, how the family shapes that culture, how the subject's traits and attitudes have been learned, how their political outlook has been shaped, how experience relates continuously from childhood to adulthood. There are ethical questions that must be considered: what should be shared, what should not, what should be guessed at, what might result from the finished work. There are dues that must be paid: to the truth, to gaps and assumptions, to the necessities of selection and design, style and form.

Clearly, a political biography is no small task to take on. Nor can it be lightly shouldered. Yet Anne Henderson's biographical essay on the life of Patrick McMahon Glynn offers a fine example of how the biographer's skills may be deployed, and what a biography may offer.

First, we should note the observant retelling of Glynn's life and recreation of his character: we see him in action, demonstrating his intelligence, ambition, persistence, optimism, and, even, his daring. Born in 1855 in the west of Ireland and educated in Gort, Dublin, and then London, Glynn emigrated to Australia at the age of twenty-five for want of work in the sector in which he was determined to make his name: the law. Despite the presence of family in Australia, this decision was no light matter. Henderson's citation of Glynn's diaries points us to Glynn's awareness that, in making the move, he was gambling: "I shake hands with the past and take my hat off to the future." It was thanks to this optimistic gamble that Glynn was able to make a decent fist of that future. His early years in Australia were hard; though he considered returning to Ireland he remained optimistic enough to seize chances when they came and make more of them than others might. His move to Kapunda – a small, out-of-the-way, district town populated mostly by farmers – would certainly have not appeared a path to easy riches; but, in retrospect, the 'Liliputian' size of that community and its lack of a blanket hostility to Catholics was instrumental to the growth of Glynn's profile. Moreover, Kapunda allowed Glynn to broaden his interests beyond legal matters. His agreement to take on the editorship of the *Kapunda Herald* in 1883 – which lent him an additional and welcome income – ensured that his knowledge of community affairs and issues increased, just as his name became better known among that community. It was almost certainly a springboard for his subsequent political career.

Henderson also takes care to reveal Glynn's character. Plutarch's reminder – that the most revealing evidence for a subject's character lies in the "casual action, the odd phrase, or a jest" – is proved in the telling details Henderson quotes. Her citation of Glynn spending Christmas Day 1881 in Melbourne's Botanic Gardens, reading Shakespeare, his "constant companion", is immensely revealing. Present in that one small line is a sense of Glynn's isolation in the new country he has come to. Also present is the glimpse of Glynn's reading tastes. He is not so interested in the passing, the easy, the lurid, or the sensational. His tastes are for the classic, the enduring, and the rewarding. There is also the hint of Glynn's inner life: though isolated, he is not lonely. He finds solace and company in Shakespeare's writings, in the depth, complexity, and richness of character and story. As other moments in Glynn's diaries show, the love of literature and reading was a persistent thread in his life. Henderson's attention to this small moment ensures that, much later, when we read of Glynn the politician, midway through a speech on water conservation, deviating to recite thirteen lines of *Troilus and Cressida*, we are not surprised; we know that it is wholly of a piece with this man, who steeps himself in classical learning and literature, who finds in it a sustenance that is also applicable to the needs of the present.

Although Glynn's achievements – his 'outstanding exploits', as Plutarch would call them – are given their due in this essay, they do not occlude that explication of Glynn himself: he is not a silhouette or a list of qualifications and offices. Henderson brings him to life. We see, in the early years after his arrival in Kapunda, Glynn's diffidence and aloofness: "With the exception of the dances, the people have kindly consented to leave me alone." We see hopes that flutter and wither, as Glynn is briefly ensorcelled by the appearance of Maggie Disher, and then transfers his interest to horses and hunting, which sustain him even in the face of failure: ". . . as long as I can keep a hunter to carry me over 1,000, 4-feet solid fences per season," he wrote in 1890, "I can drag on."

Henderson gives attention to how Glynn's beliefs and attitudes were formulated and, in turn, projected. Glynn's abiding interest in reading, and his awareness of community issues (through his work in the *Kapunda Herald*, in particular) ensured that he was engaged with the ceaseless tide of ideas and argument spreading through newspapers, periodicals, and books during the 1880s, particularly amid a wave of political and economic reform then underway in the English-speaking world. This ensured that Glynn was able to see the benefit of ideas such as the land tax, as advocated by the American economist Henry George. Henderson also points out that Glynn's receptivity to the idea was increased by his prior experiences and knowledge of Ireland, where land management and ownership laws had been of dramatic import; she adds, moreover, the resonant and significant point that, nearly simultaneous to Glynn's decision to publicly advocate for the proposal, was his willingness to call Australia home. Now, with his standing in the community established, an income (relatively) secure, and a settled knowledge that he was to stay in Australia, Glynn all but began his political career, writing the manifesto for the South Australian Land Nationalisation Society.

Henderson's discussion of the land tax, and its role in setting in motion Glynn's ejection from the South Australian parliament in 1890, is a fine example of the interplay between Glynn and his electorate. Funneled through the account of his life is a discussion of the circumstances that caused the idea to be attractive and controversial: the acute lack of government revenue in the 1880s; the fraught regulation surrounding settlement, productivity, and ownership; and the interests of the dominant farming industries. It also provides a neat intersection with Glynn's qualities of character. In a fierce election campaign, his support for the land tax left him susceptible to misrepresentation and his record to distortion. For a man wedded to the integrity of ideas and truth, these came as unexpected and, in his view, unwarranted attacks – hence his intense disappointment and outrage when he lost office and then failed, in 1893, to be elected again.

Perhaps one of the most important and laudable aspects of *Federation's Man of Letters* is the increasingly intertwined tale of Australia's federation and Glynn's advocacy and influence during that drawn-out, fraught process. Glynn's biography becomes a vehicle, during this section, by which to witness and understand the process of negotiating a constitution and system of government. Even where Glynn is unsuccessful, or his involvement appears tangential, the account of his involvement offers a much wider understanding of vital dimensions of the debate and process. His proposed amendment at the 1897 convention, to insert reference to 'Divine Providence' in the preamble, and then at the Melbourne convention in 1898 to insert a reference to divine blessing, not only alludes to Glynn's conception of God (whether his personal God or a facet of one that might stand in for all) but also another issue of contention in the colonies, one that would repeatedly surface in the century to follow – of the intersection of religion and government. Henderson's note of the campaign mounted by church groups to support references to God additionally points to the role and influence that both would exert in the newly federated country.

We may link this point to the potential of a biography to locate parallels and examples in the past that are useful or illustrative in the present. Plutarch explains the point:

> I treat the [biographical] narrative as a kind of mirror. . . . The experience is like nothing so much as spending time in their company and living with them: I receive and welcome each of them in turn as my guest, so to speak, observe "his stature

and his qualities", and choose from his achievements those which it is particularly important and valuable for me to know.

In Henderson's account of Glynn, the achievements, examples, and parallels are many. Glynn's proposal for insertion of reference to God has resonance, she argues, as the government responds to problems thrown up by the 2017 amendments to the *Marriage Act* to permit same-sex marriage. His advocacy for management of the river system in the Murray-Darling not only offers an example for how these same issues might be discussed and resolved today, but also point to the necessity and importance of compromise amid the 'political engineering' of competing interests. Glynn's caution about the expansion of the federal government and the consolidation of power previously held by the States also has uneasy parallels. Certainly, too, there are ready examples of Glynn's foresight. His view on the weaknesses reinforced by the tariff – which would become a faultline in Australian politics for the first half of the twentieth century – anticipated what became orthodox economic thought in the latter half of that century; at a time when suggestions of a return to protectionist policies are growing louder, Glynn's arguments again have force.

A final comment must be made on the form of this biography: the essay. One of the touchstones for this form is Lytton Strachey, who commends, in the oft-cited *Eminent Victorians*, the preservation of "a becoming brevity . . . that excludes everything that is redundant and nothing that is significant".[7] Strachey's argument for concision was most directed toward the biographical treatment of subjects in the Victorian era, during which lives were entombed in multiple volumes characterised by mute, respectful solemnity. Yet by arguing that biographers must distinguish between what is necessary and what is not, what is significant and not, in the story of a subject's life, Strachey was also demanding that biographers bring judgment to bear on their subjects. What he terms the biographer's "second duty", in fact, stems from so near to the first duty as to be a part of it: to "maintain his own freedom of spirit. . . . It is not his business to be complimentary; it is his business to lay bare the facts of the case, as he understands them."[8]

On the fact of it, Strachey's commendations would appear to boil down to an argument for concision, animated by sharp, independent judgment. Yet within a historical context, the ideas and example of *Eminent Victorians* recovers a model of biographical writing that had been largely eschewed in the English-speaking world since the time of James Boswell: the use of a life to address larger questions – questions that are simultaneously internal to the material (that is, to the life at hand) and extraneous to the individual. Whether those questions are didactic, comparative, illustrative, or educative is beside the point; what results from this brevity and judgment is lucid argument about the uses to which a biographer seeks to put the life of their subject.

Henderson builds from a reading of Gerald O'Collins's comprehensive *Patrick McMahon Glynn* (1965) and her own research the fine structure of a clear argument. Patrick McMahon Glynn's life, beliefs, and story are all relevant to contemporary Australia, she argues. His concerns still echo. His ideas may still bear fruit. The model he provides for integrity and intelligence is still commendable. On these points, we cannot dissent.

2. Lawyer, Catholic and liberal conservative

Anne Twomey

While he was Irish of origin, Patrick McMahon Glynn was a true South Australian. This shone through in his concern for a genuine federation in which the smaller States were not overwhelmed by the larger ones, the protection of the Murray-Darling river system,[1] which Anne Henderson has discussed in detail, and the future status of the Northern Territory of South Australia.[2]

Politically, as Henderson has observed, Glynn was a conservative and a strong supporter of free trade. Yet, at the same time, he showed a distinctly liberal streak, which was evident in his support for the right of women to vote. Glynn was not only a politician, but a lawyer of some note. This added a pragmatic aspect to how he conducted politics – he was prepared to compromise or put matters on hold, in order to achieve his goals over the long-term.

Henderson has given an admirable overview of the turns of Glynn's life, from being an educated middle-class Irish Catholic, to an impoverished Australian immigrant, to a successful lawyer, politician, and a man of public affairs. This essay seeks to supplement Henderson's work by focusing more closely on two aspects of Glynn's life. The first is the influence of religion on his political life, including the effect on his parliamentary career of his support for government grants to religious schools, his role in inserting a reference to God in the Constitution, and his efforts to remove anti-Catholic sentiment from the new King's Declaration. The second is Glynn's role as a lawyer in public affairs. He exercised his legal skills as Attorney-General both of South Australia and the Commonwealth, but narrowly missed out on appointment to the High Court of Australia.

Religious issues played a significant political role in South Australia. Glynn's support for Catholic causes, such as his objection to extending the divorce law and his support for government grants to religious schools, damaged his election prospects. During his 1890 election campaign for the electorate of Light, he had sought to overcome objections by arguing that government grants, known as 'capitation' grants, to private schools, including denominational schools, were for the purpose of supporting education, rather than religion.[3] He was, however, defeated at the poll. Henderson has discussed one reason for this loss, which concerned views attributed to Glynn regarding the taxation of land and its potential impact upon his land-owning farming constituents. But another significant contributing factor was Glynn's support for grants to denominational schools.[4]

He was therefore more circumspect in his campaign in the North Adelaide by-election of 1895, stating that the issue of capitation grants was not one that he would raise in the next session. One report even suggested that he stated he was not in favour of capitation grants,[5] but Glynn later denied this.[6] Glynn was aided in the North Adelaide by-election by the fact that it was the first occasion upon which newly enfranchised women in South Australia could vote. Glynn had been a vocal supporter of the franchise for women. He was successfully returned to Parliament, but not for long.

In 1896, at the same time as the South Australian general election, a referendum was held on the questions of whether:

(a) the system of non-religious schools established in 1891 should remain in place;

(b) whether scripture should be taught in government schools; and

(c) whether capitation grants should be made to religious schools.

This was the first referendum ever held in Australia. While proposition (a) was successful, propositions (b) and (c) were defeated by substantial margins. This suggested that the population was in favour of secular education in government schools and opposed to religious teaching in government schools and government grants to religious schools.[7] Again, this focus on religious matters may have influenced the polling in Glynn's electorate, as he lost his seat. One other factor was that during his short period in office from 1895, he had been given the task of re-writing the *Electoral Act* and he therefore felt obliged to comply with its terms, given that he had written them. Accordingly, he did not engage in paying people to canvass for him or to transport voters to polling places, unlike other less compunctious candidates.[8]

At the following general election in 1899, the issue of capitation grants for religious schools was again pushed by Catholic clerics. Glynn was annoyed by the noisy zeal of the proponents of this policy. He saw their "tactless tactics" as injuring his election chances by bringing "the secular and non-conformist elements down upon" him.[9] The other candidates were opposed to such grants. Glynn, however, gave lukewarm support. He argued that the issue of capitation grants for religious schools was not ripe, but if returned he would support a motion for a moderate grant.[10] He wrote in his diary that the issue lost him "hundreds of votes; but the better class of voters overlooked it and secured my return".[11]

His victory was again aided by the votes of women. Catherine Helen Spence, who had unsuccessfully stood as a candidate for the 1897 constitutional convention, chaired women's meetings in support of Glynn and other women canvassed for votes on his behalf.[12] Glynn had supported Spence's campaign for proportional representation, and gained Spence's support in return.[13] This was so, even though Glynn had voted in the constitutional convention against an amendment that would have required that women be given the vote in Commonwealth elections. Glynn explained to the convention that he was in favour of the enfranchisement of women, but that he did not wish to impose it on the other colonies if it would result in the loss of federation.[14] His desire to achieve federation, combined with his pragmatic view that the franchise for women across the country would eventually be won, led him to this compromise, which appears to have been accepted by his female supporters.

Glynn is most renowned, as Henderson has noted, for his pivotal role in causing reference to God to be inserted in the preamble to the *Commonwealth of Australia Constitution Act 1900*. His initial attempt to insert the phrase "invoking Divine providence" in the preamble was defeated at the Adelaide convention of 1897.[15] Edmund Barton, later to be Australia's first prime minister, had objected, noting that "there are some occasions on which the invocation of the Deity is more reverently left out than made". He did not think it was up to the framers of the Constitution to judge whether voters went to the polls to approve federation while invoking Divine providence, and this was certainly not a judgment that could be made before the poll was even held.[16] He implied that it would be wrong to commence the Constitution with a falsehood, albeit a pious one.

Glynn, however, was undeterred. Supported by a large number of public petitions and recommendations from colonial legislatures, he returned to the convention in Melbourne in 1898 with a revised proposal. This time he had consulted the drafting committee to ensure that it was phrased in the "least objectionable" manner.[17] Glynn moved that the words "humbly relying upon the blessing of Almighty God" be inserted in the preamble. He observed that these words were "simple and unsectarian". He revealed, in his speech, his inner thinking and his deep commitment to religion by observing that this phrase was "expressive of our ultimate hope of the final end of all our aspirations, of the great elemental truth upon which all our creeds are based, and towards which the lines of our faiths converge".[18]

Glynn also saw this phrase as a unifying one that would sink the differences of religious form and method and give rise to a "spirit of toleration" that would grow strong under a common aim.[19] Glynn, who was well known for his love of Shakespeare, poetry, and literature, and who could quote enormous slabs of it from memory, waxed lyrically upon the role of religion in public life:

> It is this, not the iron hand of the law, that is the bond of society; it is this that gives unity and tone to the texture of the whole; it is this, that by subduing the domineering impulses and the reckless passions of the heart, turns discord to harmony, and evolves the law of moral progress out of the clashing purposes of life.[20]

Glynn saw a reference to God in the preamble as an antidote

to cynicism and materialism, as it "may at times remind us of ideals beyond the counter, and of hopes that lift us higher than the vulgar realities of the day".[21]

While Glynn was operating on a higher plain in proposing the insertion of these words, others, such as the Victorian lawyer Henry Bournes Higgins, who was later to become a Justice of the High Court, worried that such words could be dangerous if there were not a sufficient safeguard to prevent the Commonwealth Parliament from enacting laws concerning religious matters, such as the closing of shops on Sunday to ensure Christian observances.[22] These were matters that should be left to the States. A consequence, as pointed out by Henderson, was the enactment of section 116 of the Constitution which expressly limits the Commonwealth Parliament's powers with respect to religion.

Others were concerned that the words were really a sham in their implication of unfounded piety. The former premier of Tasmania, Adye Douglas, was the most brutal in his criticism, observing:

> What is the object of inserting these words? Is it to make the people believe that they will be more religious if the words are inserted? Shall we be more religious if we put them in? Will it have any effect whatever upon us? Why, it is all nonsense – a sham and a delusion – like many other things that have taken place here! I presume that I am ordinarily as religious as any member of this Convention, but I do not make a parade of it.[23]

Douglas added that the insertion of these words would "be a mockery" and that it would "minister to hypocrisy".[24] He urged delegates to vote against the amendment. Nonetheless, this time Glynn was successful. The strong popular support for the change, evidenced by petitions from across the various colonies, was sufficient to spur delegates to support the change.

The result was that the Act of the Westminster Parliament – the *Commonwealth of Australia Constitution Act 1900* – which in section 9 sets out the Commonwealth Constitution, commences with a preamble asserting that the "people of New South Wales, Victoria, South Australia, Queensland and Tasmania, humbly relying on the blessing of Almighty God, have agreed to unite in one indissoluble Federal Commonwealth under the Crown of the United Kingdom of Great Britain and Ireland, and under the Constitution hereby established".[25]

Glynn was both a loyal Irish Catholic and a supporter of the Crown. He did not regard the two as inconsistent. Henderson has rightly observed that "his support for the Crown was unambiguous". Upon the death of King Edward VII, Glynn and a number of other Members of the House of Representatives supported a humble address to the new King, expressing "unswerving loyalty and devotion" and petitioning a change in the Declaration to be made by the new Sovereign so as to remove parts that were offensive to Catholics. The existing Declaration, as imposed by the *Act of Settlement 1689*, required the King to declare, amongst other things, that "the invocation or adoration of the Virgin Mary or any other saint, and the sacrifice of the Mass, as they are now used in the Church of Rome, are superstitious and idolatrous".

As Henderson has discussed, Glynn regarded such a Declaration as no longer appropriate. He observed that the "spirit of intolerance . . . is not the spirit of our days" and that we now "recognise in our laws and institutions . . . that the worth of a man, as subject and citizen, does not depend on the accident of his birth or creed".[26] He also pointed out that the faith that was the subject of obloquy in the Declaration, was "the faith of England for nearly a thousand years – the faith of the founder of that Abbey in which the Kings and Queens of England, Catholic and Protestant alike, are buried".[27] The House ended up adopting an amendment moved by Sir John Quick for the House to approve of changes to the Declaration as suggested by the prime minister of the United Kingdom, which reduced its length, having the effect of excluding the offensive references to Catholic doctrine.[28] The Declaration was duly altered by the *Accession Declaration Act 1910*.[29]

Glynn found his identity not only in his faith as a Catholic, but his work as a lawyer. He obtained a Bachelor of Arts from Trinity College Dublin and studied law at the Middle Temple in London.[30] His early life as a barrister in Ireland was unsuccessful, and he was even less successful when admitted to the bar in Melbourne. Selling sewing machines initially proved more profitable to him than the practice of law. But he eventually gained work as a solicitor in a country town in South Australia, later becoming a successful lawyer and being appointed a King's Counsel in July 1913. Glynn was most known, however, for his legal work as a politician, initially in the South Australian House of Assembly, including a very short stint as Attorney-General in the Solomon Ministry. His prominence earned him election, as an independent, to the constitutional convention of 1897-98, where he threw himself into the detail of draft provisions and their amendment. Later, he fulfilled the important role of Commonwealth Attorney-General from 1909-10.[31]

At the Constitutional Convention of 1897, Glynn was a member of the Judiciary Committee. Glynn considered that the establishment of a new High Court for Australia would be an extravagance. He argued both at the convention,[32] and in the Commonwealth Parliament,[33] that the High Court should instead be comprised of State judges, such as the Chief Justice from each State, to save expense, at least until the Court had sufficient work of its own to justify the full-time appointment of new judges. Despite his views, the High Court was established with its own Justices in 1903.

In November 1912, after the death of Justice O'Connor, rumours circulated that Glynn might be appointed to the High Court in his place.[34] Glynn did not appear particularly enthusiastic at the prospect. He noted in his diary that there was greater attraction in making the law, rather than interpreting it, so he was not pursuing the role.[35] But with the passage of a Bill to allow the appointment of an additional two Justices, creating three vacancies in total, it was reported that Glynn was "regarded as a certainty for elevation to the Bench".[36]

This was so, even though Glynn was a Conservative free trader, albeit with a liberal ilk, and it was the Fisher Labor government that was making the appointments. After Frank Gavan Duffy was appointed, leaving two vacancies yet to be filled, speculation about Glynn's future appointment continued:

> In well-informed circles, it is stated that Mr Glynn would have received the first offer, but from the fact that he is at present engaged . . . in drafting in behalf of the Liberal Party their view with regard to the proposed alteration to the Constitution. So far as can be learned members of the Cabinet did not consider that it would be fair to the Opposition to deprive them of Mr Glynn's legal experience at this stage.[37]

It is hard to imagine a government today appointing an

opposition member to the High Court, or the possibility that the appointment would be delayed so as not to unfairly deprive the opposition of legal advice. Nonetheless, Glynn was not appointed, and the reason attributed to this failure was generally political. In one newspaper, it was observed that if it were a matter for the Labor Caucus, "the probabilities are that Mr Glynn would be selected", but that he had opponents within the Ministry, including one particular member whose opinion carried "no end of weight".[38] Another critic was the Chief Justice of South Australia, Sir John Gordon, who rejected the offer of appointment himself and wrote to the Attorney-General noting that Glynn was a "good fellow" but that his mental output resembled "scrambled eggs – wholesome enough, but messy".[39]

Others claimed that at the time he was about to be appointed, he destroyed his chances by making a controversial speech on the second reading of the referendum bill.[40] In *Punch*, it was observed that Glynn "has the consolation of knowing that he narrowly missed being such an extraordinarily exceptional man that his political opponents promoted him to the highest judiciary appointment in the Commonwealth".[41] As late as 1920, Glynn's name was still being mentioned as a prospective appointment to the High Court.[42]

While Glynn is not the most prominent of the framers of the Constitution, as Henderson has discussed, he made significant contributions both to the drafting of the Constitution and in giving effect to it in the first two decades of the Commonwealth's existence. No doubt he could have made an even greater contribution on the High Court if given the opportunity, but he will continue to be known for his legal acumen, his persistence, his fairness, and his faith.

3. Personality and prejudice: Glynn and Isaacs compared

Suzanne D. Rutland

In her biography of Patrick McMahon Glynn, Anne Henderson described him as "the most significant Catholic figure to have risen on the non-Labor side of Australian politics." The same could be said of Sir Isaac Isaacs, who was by far the leading Jewish personality in Australian politics in the period of Federation. There are significant synergies between the biographies of the two men. Both men came from immigrant backgrounds, both were trained in the law and both struggled to establish themselves. Above all, both men belonged to minority groups which experienced significant prejudice, bigotry and discrimination in Australia – Glynn as an Irish Catholic and Isaacs as a member of the Jewish community. Yet, both men were able to succeed due their personal abilities due to their erudition and their capacity for hard work and the greater freedom offered in Australian colonial society and to make their mark on Australian history and constitutional law.

Sir Isaac Alfred Isaacs was born in Melbourne in 1855, son of a poor immigrant family from Poland and England. Just as Glynn, who was born just a few days later, migrated to Australia in search of a better life, Isaac's father, Alfred, a tailor, left his small town of Mlava in the Russian section of Poland for a better life, arriving first in England, where he married Rebecca Abrahams, a very strong woman with whom Isaacs remained close for the rest of his life. They decided to emigrate from there to Australia in 1854, attracted by the news of the gold rush in Victoria.[1] Even though Isaacs was born in Australia, unlike Glynn who arrived as a twenty-five-year-old man, he would have been very aware of his immigrant background and the struggle which his parents faced. As with Glynn, they moved to the country in 1859 in order to establish themselves and this is where Isaacs grew up.

Just as Glynn faced great difficulties in building his career in Australia, so did Isaacs. He began his career as a teacher at Yackandandah and Beechworth state schools, and then entered the civil service while studying law at night. As a brilliant student, he graduated with first class honours in 1880, and later gained his Master of Arts degree. In 1882, he was admitted to the bar and took silk in 1899. He also combined his career in law with his political involvement, initially at the colonial level. From 1892 to 1901, he represented the electorate of Bogong, which included the areas around Yackandandah and Beechworth in Victoria. However, he did not experience the same setbacks that Glynn did in this period. He served as Solicitor-General from 1892 and Attorney-General from 1894 to 1899.

Isaacs was successful due to his combination of erudition and an outstanding ability for hard work – qualities he shared with Glynn. He was a considerable scholar and linguist who was also noted for his persistence. Sir Robert Gratton, who was secretary to the Attorney-General's Department, described Isaacs as follows:

> [Isaacs'] capacity for work was amazing. By day he carried on the biggest practice of the Victorian Bar; by night he did full justice to the duties of Attorney-General.

He sometimes slept, I must believe, though I could never discover when. I once left him at the office at midnight, and on my way home took to the printer a draft bill that was to be ready in the morning. Coming to the office early, I found on my table an envelope from the Government Printer, containing an entirely different draft, which, in some wonderment, I took in to the Attorney. He confessed that in the small hours he had had a new inspiration, and had recovered the draft from the printer, and had reshaped it, lock, stock and barrel.[2]

It was these qualities which contributed to his success, despite the issues of prejudice and discrimination due to the Protestant dominance in Australian society. Isaacs was born three years before the first Jew, Baron Lionel de Rothschild, was able to take his seat in the Westminster parliament in 1858, because he refused to swear his oath of allegiance on the New Testament, as required up until then. Benjamin Disraeli had converted to Christianity and so was able to take on a leading role in British politics despite his Jewish origins. While he was not religious, Isaacs was acutely aware of his Jewish background throughout his career and never sought to hide this, despite the antisemitism which he experienced.

As Frank Fletcher, has shown, antisemitism emerged in Australia in the late nineteenth century, due to the emerging Australian nationalism (particularly after 1880), the fear of a flood of foreign East European Jews as a result of the Tsarist pogroms, and the severe impact of the depression of the 1890s.[3] Even though the number of Jewish refugees from Russia was tiny compared to the two million who sought a new life in the United States – the *Goldene Medina* – there was a strong antisemitic outcry against their arrival in Australia. This was particularly so when it was mooted that Baron de Hirsch wished to promote Jewish settlements there. Anti-Jewish immigration sentiment was expressed by trade unions, some politicians, and in the general press. *The Bulletin* and *Truth* both highlighted the economic peculiarities of Jews, and during the Russian immigration scare *The Bulletin* commented:

> Even the Chinaman is cheaper in the end than the Hebrew . . . the one with the tail is preferable to the one with the Talmud every time. We owe much to the Jew – in more sense than one – but until he works, until a fair percentage of him produces, he must always be against democracy.[4]

Given the strength of anti-Chinese sentiment in Australia at the time, this was a very strong statement, reflecting contemporary attitudes towards Jews who were seen as only concerned with money, creating urban clusters, sticking together, and being clannish.

Hilary Rubinstein points out that the jibes in some papers, particularly *Punch*, which in one cartoon highlighted the claim that Jews and lawyers dominated the Victorian Legislative Assembly – and Isaacs was both – were often satirical and so should not be taken too seriously. However, she argues that "malevolence and not mere mischief seems to have motivated some of its contributions made at Jewish expense" and that this applied to the "venomous attacks on Jewry" seen in the writings of Marcus Clarke.[5]

While anti-Catholic and anti-Jewish sentiments at this time did not exclude Jews from taking on leadership roles in politics, they were excluded from many upper-class institutions, in what might be called a 'gentleman's racism'. This social exclusion manifested itself very specifically in the policies of the top golf clubs, even though there is no evidence of such exclusion from most other sports in Australia. Thus, in 1908, the Royal Sydney Golf Club passed a resolution excluding Jews, even though Jews had previously been permitted to join, and these exclusionary policies also applied to Catholics. Colin Tatz points out that as late as the 1960s, Bonnie Doon's membership criterion was paraphrased as "No Jews, jockeys or Catholics".[6] These discriminatory policies led both Catholics and Jews to form their own golf clubs – for Jews it was the Monash Country Club, opened in 1931, and in Melbourne the Cranbourne Country Club. Clearly, both Glynn and Isaacs were aware of this prejudice and discrimination, leading them to advocate more liberal views, even though both were on the conservative side of government and both served under Deakin as Attorney-General.

Isaacs played a prominent role in the movement for federation and in 1897 was chosen as one of the ten Victorian representatives to the federal convention, being elected in fifth place. His positions on most issues reflected the general approach of Victoria, where the desire for federation was strong, whereas in New South Wales, the only colony that supported free trade, opinion was divided because of the fear that federation would interfere with its economic interests. Isaacs was supported by co-religionist Vaiben L. Solomon of South Australia, in contrast to Sir Julian Salomons, who opposed federation as disadvantageous to the interests of New South Wales.[7]

After Federation, Isaacs entered the federal parliament, representing Indi, located in North-Eastern Victoria, from 1901 to 1906, including his period as Attorney-General in 1905-6. He was appointed Attorney-General in the Second Deakin Ministry.

Glynn and Isaacs crossed paths in relation to Murray River riparian rights. As Henderson discusses, Glynn was asked to prepare a brief on the right of the States to the Murray waters, while Isaacs accepted a retainer from the South Australian government in his private capacity as a leading barrister for the South Australian government. Glynn's detailed two-volume case was submitted to Isaacs and Josiah Symon, the federal Attorney-General at the time. They conferred with Glynn in late 1905 to 1906, by which time Isaacs had replaced Symon as Attorney-General. Cowen argues that except in some marginal matters they "supported Glynn's case for riparian rights".[8]

As Henderson makes clear, Glynn was "a well-loved and attractive individual" while Isaacs often antagonised people. In the late 1890s, Alfred Deakin noted that Isaac was known for his verbose and rhetorical speaking style and his strong conviction of his own infallibility. He wrote about Isaacs:

> A clear, cogent, fiery speaker, he set himself at once to work to conquer the methods of platform and parliamentary debate and in both succeeded. He was not trusted or liked in the House. His will was indomitable, his courage inexhaustible and his ambition immeasurable. But his egotism was too marked and his ambition too ruthless to render him popular. Dogmatic by disposition, full of legal subtlety and the precise literalness and littleness of the rabbinic mind, he was at the same time kept well abreast by his reading of modern developments and modern ideas.[9]

These comments sum up Isaacs's strengths and weaknesses. His intellectual brilliance and reformist policies won him support, but not personal liking. His unpopularity cannot be traced merely to jealousy or antisemitism, but was a result of his dogmatism, which at times led to controversy within the Jewish community as well. The greatest division he created within the Jewish community was over Deakin's proposal for a referendum to introduce general scripture lessons based on the Christian faith. Both Isaacs and Theodore Fink, another Jewish parliamentarian, voted in support of the proposal, much to the chagrin of the Jewish community.

In terms of Deakin's reference to the "littleness of the rabbinic mind", it is difficult to ascertain to what extent this had a tinge of antisemitism in it, and to what extent it was a reaction to Isaacs' dogmatic personality. However, as seen in the quote above from *The Bulletin*, the Talmud, which did not form part of Christian beliefs of practice, was viewed very critically so that it was often part of antisemitic discourse.

In contrast, it is clear that Deakin's description of Glynn, as quoted by Henderson, was much more positive. Clearly Glynn was a popular figure, whereas Isaacs had a tendency to alienate people, particularly during the federation debates when, as Cowen explained, "his long expositions and analyses wearied both lawyer and non-lawyer members of the convention". Interestingly, Cowen chooses an example from Glynn, whom he describes as "a man of considerable legal, constitutional and general knowledge" as an example of this alienation.[10] The matter of debate related to a constitutional issue regarding the Commonwealth's liability in contract and tort, a proposal which Isaac strongly opposed. In support of his argument, Glynn gave an American case, to which Isaacs interjected:

> Mr Isaacs: Does the honourable member refer to the case of *Chisholm v Georgia*, when the Supreme Court decided

that a state could be sued under the Constitution? It required the eleventh amendment to reverse that.

Mr Glynn: A man would have to live to the age of Methuselah to cultivate a memory equal to remembering all the cases to which the honourable member is always referring.[11]

This is but one example of a point of disagreement between the two men. It is a telling example, however, because it reveals the pedantry of Isaacs, which alienated colleagues and reinforced prejudices, and the humour of Glynn, which endeared him to colleagues and helped break down prejudices.

More importantly from a political perspective, whilst Isaac was a strong supporter of federation, he was also strongly in support of protectionism. When he stood for election for the Bogong electorate, he promoted both federalism and protectionism, reflecting the overall attitudes of the Victorian legislature, which had introduced high tariffs to protect Victorian industries.[12] Yet, during the parliamentary debates after federation, Cowen argues that Isaacs was not an active proponent of tariffs, although he did refer to free trade as a "dying faith" and provided detailed examples of how it had a negative effect on the working class because industries needed protection.[13] In this regard, he took a very different position from Glynn.

The same applied to the issue of establishing a federal supreme court, to be known as the High Court of Australia. Glynn, together with another leading lawyer, Henry Bournes Higgins, believed that the government should wait to establish the High Court, while Isaacs strongly disagreed. In this argument, he firmly supported Deakin, who served as Attorney-General under Edmund Barton, Australia's first prime minister. The bill was passed into law in 1903, following "a difficult and complex debate" with the attacks being "led by Higgins and Glynn . . . [who argued that] the Judicial Committee of the Privy Council on appeal, could adequately discharge the role contemplated for the High Court".[14]

After serving as Attorney-General from 1905-6, in 1906 Isaac was appointed to the High Court, where he served with distinction for twenty-four years. Interestingly, Higgins also served as Attorney-General and was also appointed to the High Court in the same year as Isaacs, serving on the court until his death in 1927. Isaacs was eventually promoted to chief justice in 1930. Six months later, he was appointed Australia's first native-born governor-general, serving in this position for six years. Isaacs died in 1948, aged ninety-two years.

In the last years of his life, Isaacs found himself in conflict with the Jewish community over political Zionism. In 1917, Arthur Balfour, then British foreign secretary, sent a letter to Lord Rothschild, which recognised the right of the Jewish people to establish a national homeland in Palestine. The subsequent British mandate, which was based on what became known as the Balfour Declaration, resulted in the Australian Jewish leadership initially not opposing Zionism. One editor explained: "We have yet to learn that while Britain holds the mandate for Palestine and while Britain favours the development of a Jewish homeland there can be any lack of patriotism in being a Zionist".[15]

As tensions rapidly developed between the Jewish settlement in Palestine and the British, most Anglo-Jews in Australia withdrew their support for the Zionist movement.[16] In their effort to become fully integrated into Australian society, the Anglo-Jewish establishment assumed a policy of being more

British than the British. When faced with a conflict between Britain and the Jewish settlement, they supported Britain. Thus, the mainstream position of Australian Jewry was based more on pragmatic considerations than with concerns about dual loyalty.

In contrast to this pragmatic approach, Isaacs supported the strong ideological position of those British rabbinical and lay leaders who opposed the Zionist concepts on the basis that Judaism was a religion and not a nationality. He saw himself as British by nationality and Jewish by religion, despite the fact that he himself was not strictly observant according to Orthodox Jewish practice. As tensions between the Jewish settlers and the British mandatory authorities increased, so did his rhetoric against what he referred to in a 1937 letter to his family as "dangerous Zionist" doctrines.[17] Like Glynn, Isaacs felt a strong sense of British patriotism. Whereas Glynn felt able to support Irish home rule and to criticise British policies without compromising his loyalty to the British Empire, Isaacs appears to have felt criticism of British policy was incompatible with loyalty to the British Empire in a way that Glynn did not.

From 1941 onwards, Isaac mounted a campaign against what he called "extreme Zionism", particularly following the British White Paper of 1939, which limited Jewish migration to an annual quota of 75,000 for five years, ending any hope of a Jewish homeland and leading to widespread protest from Zionist organisations. In 1941 he set out his reasons for objecting to the establishment of a Jewish state: it would be unjust to the million Arabs living there, "would imperil the safety of places and structures as sacred to the Christian and Muslim worlds as to Jews and further, would so arouse the antagonism of the Muslim world as to endanger the security and integrity of the Empire".[18]

This was an opening salvo of three years of polemics against the Zionist movement, which in 1943 were rebutted by the young jurist, Professor Julius Stone, who had been appointed to his professorship at the University of Sydney. Stone's arguments were published by the Zionist movement in a booklet entitled *Stand Up and Be Counted* in 1944.[19]

Of the prominent Jewish figures of this period, the two outstanding names by far are Sir Isaac Isaacs and Sir John Monash. Indeed, the story is told that when the Australian prime minister, James Scullin, went to advise the King, who subsequently appointed the first Australian-born governor-general, he had two names in his pocket – Isaacs and Monash. Their success represented what Colin Tatz has described "as the yardstick of the Australian fair go, the land where discrimination doesn't exist, where Jews were able to participate in the political, legal, economic, and cultural life of the land."[20] Whilst this was a somewhat mythical picture, since prejudice and discrimination against both Jews and Catholics did exist, it certainly applied to the successful legal and political careers of both Isaacs and Glynn. Isaacs's story also suggests some degree of meritocracy existed, given that he could flourish despite the way in which his personality may have compounded his colleagues' prejudices.

4. Anglican elites

Peter Boyce

Anne Henderson's assessment of Patrick McMahon Glynn's sterling service to Australian national politics from the 1890s and through the Great War also highlights his serious allegiance to the Catholic faith, and this in a period of Anglican numerical and socio-political dominance which survived until the second half of the twentieth century.

On the eve of Federation, Catholics, mostly of Irish origin, represented some 23 per cent of Australian Christians, and two-thirds of their priests were Irish-born. No Australian-born Catholic bishop was appointed until 1942. Although Anglicanism was never the formally established church in Australia's six colonies, it was frequently treated by colonial governors, some bishops, and even the Colonial Office in London, as if it were. The Church of England had been 'established' in 1534, following King Henry's breach with Rome, and Anglicanism in colonial Australia was its constitutional appendage, as in Canada, New Zealand, and South Africa. Under pressure from the then Archbishop of Canterbury (Geoffrey Fisher), the Church of England in Australia, as it was formally known, adopted its own national constitution in 1961 and subsequently amended its title to 'the Anglican Church of Australia'. Anglicans remained the largest category of Australian Christians until 1984, when overtaken by Catholics.

During Glynn's thirty-year political career, Anglicans were

still plentifully represented in the rural gentry, the judiciary, the military, and conservative politics. Bishops and other senior clergy were still imported from Britain and frequently were graduates of Oxford or Cambridge University, socially linked to Government House, and ardent advocates of empire. They enjoyed high rank in official tables of precedence and their metropolitan cathedrals hosted major state ceremonies. A minority of clergy were 'high church' Anglo-Catholics, influenced by the Tractarian Movement of the 1830s, who tended to favour strong welfare programs for working-class parishioners.

The Anglican clerical leadership were not, on the whole, ill-disposed to Roman Catholics, but the 1916 Easter Uprising in Dublin and the widespread lack of enthusiasm among Irish Australians for the imperial military effort during the Great War drew fire from some Anglican leaders. On the other hand, because so many Irish Australians had been born and raised in the Australian colonies, they had developed strong nationalist sentiments and were willing to support the war effort.

Although Irish immigrant Catholics were not systematically discriminated against, they were often overlooked for recruitment or promotion in senior public sector appointments, and their political party of choice tended to be Labor. The attitudes of practising Anglicans towards the Irish Catholic minority varied considerably from diocese to diocese because of the variety of doctrinal positions and governance structures between Australian dioceses, of which there were already more than twenty. The diocese of Adelaide, in which Glynn resided in his early Australian years, was one of the country's most tolerant. The diocese most suspicious of Catholic worship, Sydney, was already dominated by a rather severe evangelical outlook and boasted several battalions of vocal Protestant Ulstermen (opposed to the establishment of an independent Irish state). In several other dioceses, including Perth, Brisbane, and Tasmania, Anglican-Catholic relations were more harmonious. But such harmony was not yet infused with any ecumenical spirit. It was a climate of peaceful co-existence, not of shared worship or even vigorous intellectual discourse. Ecumenism had to wait until the 1960s.

The initial rejection of Glynn's historic motion to incorporate acknowledgment of God's benign sovereignty in the Constitution's preamble ("humbly relying on the blessing of Almighty God") may not have been related to any suspicion of the motion's sponsor. One of the two delegates who spoke against it was Sir Edward Braddon, Tasmanian premier and an Anglican lay leader in his diocese. Braddon was a delegate to the Anglican synod during the 1890s, and sometimes rejected the conservative stand of evangelical synodsmen on contentious social issues, including his government's decision to approve the opening of Tattersall's lottery in Tasmania. As a graduate of Trinity College Dublin (one of Britain's seven 'ancient' universities, founded by the first Queen Elizabeth), Glynn would have been no stranger to the company of cultivated Anglicans. At the time of his enrolment, Catholics needed permission from the Catholic authorities, a restriction which remained in place until 1970.

As the only Catholic in W. M. Hughes's Nationalist Party cabinet, Glynn endorsed the prime minister's vigorous prosecution of Australia's war effort. This included the cause of conscription during the two referenda of 1916-17. He was undaunted by the public opposition vented by Melbourne's fiery Catholic archbishop, Daniel Mannix, but was not necessarily sympathetic to the anti-Catholic jibes of some of Melbourne's regular Protestant polemicists, including the warden of Melbourne University's Trinity College, Alexander Leeper. A respected classical scholar, Leeper was the product of an 'Anglo-Irish ascendancy' family, and his public denunciations of Mannix were joined with others from the Victorian Protestant Federation and Orange lodges.* We should note, however, that a few Catholic prelates endorsed conscription, including Sydney's archbishop, Michael Kelly, and Perth's archbishop, Patrick Clune. The latter boasted a friendship with his Anglican opposite-number, archbishop C. O. L. Riley, and they served together as chaplains-general to the Australian Imperial Force.

Community attitudes to Australian residents who publicly sympathised with Germany during the Great War could be harsh, none more so than calls for deportation of the German priest, Charles Jerger. His eventual deportation in 1920, despite appeals on his behalf in cabinet by Glynn, does not seem to have been influenced by agitation from Anglicans. Some Catholics, as well as Methodist and Presbyterian critics, apparently led the charge.

Glynn's career in federal politics ended with his loss of a seat in the 1919 election (which followed Hughes's defection to the Labor Party). During the interwar years, the climate of suspicion against Catholicism in Australia weakened, especially in the wake of immigration to Australia from non-Irish Catholic sources. Irish independence from 1923 (though still nominally under the Crown) removed one of the root causes of Protestant

---

* Orange lodges were masonic associations of northern Irishmen honouring the defeat in battle of England's fugitive Catholic king, James II, by his Protestant successor, William of Orange, in 1690.

distrust, and by the outbreak of the World War II, Catholics were edging closer to numerical equivalence with Anglicans. From the late 1940s, Protestant clergy were beginning to develop a strong ecumenical spirit (at least among themselves), assisted by the establishment of the World Council of Churches. But Catholics remained aloof from this movement until encouraged by the Second Vatican Council (1962-5). From the late 1960s, there was more conspicuous evidence of Catholic leadership in theological scholarship and public discussion. This writer sadly recalls that in the mid-1950s, in the closing days of a visit to Australia by the secretary-general of the World Council of Churches, W. A. Visser't Hooft (a distinguished Dutch theologian), the visitor confessed to him privately that his most striking and troubling impression of Australian Christianity was "the anti-intellectualism of the Catholic clergy". Because Visser't Hooft worked closely with Dutch and Belgian church leaders, especially Cardinal Suenens, the ecumenical primate of Belgium, the contrast would have been stark. But the Dutch visitor's harsh verdict would have been less justifiable twenty years later. By the 1970s, Catholic leadership in the public service and the universities had become more pronounced. Indeed, by early 1996, the three most senior public offices in Australia were occupied by Catholics concurrently – Sir William Deane as governor-general, Paul Keating as prime minister and Sir Gerard Brennan as chief justice of the High Court.

The conservative decade following the World War witnessed sustained support for the mainstream Christian churches in Australia, measured by statistics of membership and church attendance. But from the 1960s, the Anglicans began to suffer a steady decline. Catholicism benefitted from both European immigration and a higher birth rate, and in 1984 the Anglicans lost their majority. The decline of Anglicanism was obviously affected by the global spread of secularism and a generally weak record of local evangelism, but the structure of Anglican governance would exacerbate the problem from the 1990s. Australian Anglicanism emphasizes the independence of each diocese under its episcopal leadership, allowing dioceses to establish distinctive traditions of church worship and even doctrine, monitored and validated by the bishop's standing committee, the diocesan council, which can be tightly controlled. Most of Australia's twenty-three dioceses have not been permanently tied to any one school of churchmanship, remaining sufficiently 'broad' or 'liberal' to permit the co-existence of both evangelical and non-evangelical practices, but a few dioceses, most notably and problematically the archdiocese of Sydney, have created a deep constitutional and cultural divide within Australian Anglicanism.

Sydney became identified as an evangelical diocese during the second half of the nineteenth century, following the establishment of Moore College as the centre of theological training for its clergy. During the next century, the lengthy tenures of T. C. Hammond (1936-53) and D. Broughton Knox (1959-85) as principal helped confirm the Sydney archdiocese as a powerful generator of conservative evangelicalism in the world-wide Anglican communion, with particular emphasis on the primacy of clerical preaching (at the expense of liturgy, formal prayers, and choral music), a tendency to interpret scripture literally, and a strong emphasis on mission. Hammond, in particular, was publicly scornful of Roman Catholicism and he also abhorred high-church Anglicanism (Anglo-Catholicism).

These developments in Sydney were carried a step further with the election of Peter Jensen (then principal of Moore College) as archbishop in 2001 and Jensen's immediate appointment of his brother Phillip as dean of St Andrew's Cathedral. The politics behind the Jensen election involved lobbying and head-counting on a scale hitherto unknown in Australian Anglicanism, a political saga well documented by Chris McGillion in *The Chosen Ones: The Politics of Salvation in the Anglican Church.* A serious consequence of the Jensen ascendancy was the strain soon imposed on Anglicanism's national legislature, General Synod, whose canons and rules are intended for adoption by all twenty-three dioceses. Because Sydney is the largest and wealthiest diocese, its political clout must be taken very seriously if schism is to be avoided. One defensive weapon still available to the non-evangelical majority of dioceses is their influence in electing the church's primate. No archbishop of Sydney is likely to be elected primate in the foreseeable future.

While conservative evangelicalism in Sydney is not a publicly declared enemy of Catholicism, the fundamentals of Catholic teaching and worship are still unwelcome – the two chief obstacles being Catholicism's authoritarian structure and its alleged claim to a monopoly of truth. As recently as 1970, Archbishop Marcus Loane refused to participate in a public ceremony of greeting for the visiting pope, Paul VI. On the other hand, Jensen agreed to launch a biography of Cardinal George Pell more than two decades later.

In the past decade, Jensen and his successor, Archbishop Glenn Davies, have helped launch and finance an international revisionist movement aimed at purifying the world-wide Anglican communion from liberalism, focusing on sexuality and gender issues. GAFCON (Global Anglican Futures Conference) boycotted the 2008 Lambeth Conference (hosted every ten years by Anglicanism's spiritual leader, the Archbishop of Canterbury), and has threatened to boycott the forthcoming 2020 conference. GAFCON's supporters constitute the Fellowship of Confessing Anglicans, whose current Australian chairman is the bishop of Tasmania, Richard Condie. The bulk of GAFCON's episcopal leadership is drawn from large west and east African dioceses, where homosexuality is not tolerated. These countries now contain the majority of the world's communicant Anglicans. It is believed that the Sydney diocese has helped fund the travel costs of African bishops attending GAFCON conferences in Jerusalem. GAFCON's Australian leaders have also declared an eagerness to 'plant churches' in dioceses where liberalism has taken hold, and they claim eligibility to do so without permission from the local bishop.

Conservative evangelicals in Australia do not seem to feel the need to publicly defend their distinctive portrayal of Anglicanism, but in September 2011, a Moore College theology lecturer, Michael Jensen, devoted an episode of the ABC's *Religion and Ethics* program to the question "Are Sydney Anglicans actually Anglican?" Not surprisingly, he claimed that the new presentation of Anglicanism in Sydney was loyal to the Church of England's sixteenth-century Protestant roots, but instead of the church boasting its role as the *via media* between Catholicism and Protestantism, the legitimate *via media* for Jensen was between Martin Luther's Wittenberg and John Calvin's Geneva. Jensen emphasized evangelicalism's recognition of Scripture as the "supreme authority" and its commitment to conversionism (i.e. its missionary role). He relegated matters of clerical dress to being of secondary importance, even though the diocese has prohibited the wearing of Eucharistic vestments since 1910. Jensen's was not a charitable or reassuring message, and he dismissed non-evangelicals as "liberal-Catholics" who "expect to be in charge of things".

Meanwhile, the spirit and discipline of Sydney Anglicanism has spread to several other Australian dioceses – Tasmania among them. There, the bishop upset thousands of the faithful in 2018 by demanding the sale of more than seventy historic churches to raise funds for a redress scheme for victims of clerical sexual abuse. But only one-quarter of the sums demanded were to be allocated to redress. The remainder would be used to restructure parishes in ways not yet specified.

Anglicanism may no longer be recognised as a *via media*, but its history reveals a strong mediating tradition. The distinguished Cambridge theologian, Alec Vidler, has argued that "Anglican theology is true to its genius when it is seeking to resolve opposed systems", and a contemporary Australian scholar, Randall Nolan, entitled his doctoral thesis, "A Mediating Tradition: The Anglican Vocation in Australian Society". Meanwhile, the numbers of Australians identifying as Anglicans or Catholics continue to slide. The 2016 census revealed that only 22.6 per cent were Catholic and 13.3 per cent Anglican. Since then, both church families have been wracked by clergy abuse scandals – a far cry from the era of Anglican elitism and the Catholic struggle for status so familiar to Patrick McMahon Glynn.

5. Now and then

John Fahey

As a lawyer, I studied constitutional law in 1964. I remember learning about Deakin, Parkes, and Barton, but I confess that I never really knew about the role of many others, including Glynn. I have cribbed occasionally, and enjoyed quoting him on the miseries of Melbourne to goad the vice-chancellor, who still seems to glory in some reverie of Marvellous Melbourne. It was only when I read Anne Henderson's essay that I felt that I had found out who Glynn was, and that I really got to know him for the first time. Glynn's name should have been up in lights and it should have been known to me. He was a man of substance who deserves to be written not only into history, but into the school curriculum. What I take from Henderson's essay is the picture of a man who tried to make a difference, and whose legacy can still be felt a century later. His story involves issues that we still face – not least racism and bigotry. In this brief reflection, I should like to consider three topics: what it means to be a Catholic in public life; what it means to contribute to public debate; and what it means to have a commitment to Australia. Glynn's life reveals insights into these three topics relevant to our understanding of them now and then.

Glynn was not what I would call a 'prominent Catholic'. When you look at what he said and did, you can see the influence of his Catholic education, but he did not pin anything he said or did in public life on the teachings of the church. I would say that the teachings of the church provided a moral compass for him. That said, he seems to have been happy enough to express criticism of the church when he thought people within it fell short of the mark. We see a lot of this today – that Catholic values provide a moral compass for leadership. This is part of the church's legacy that is often overlooked.

There is a tendency to label people as 'good Catholics' if they go to Mass on Sunday and to label people as 'nominal Catholics' if they do not. What is more important, however, is that a Catholic's moral compass is informed by Catholic values. So I believe that we need to be more tolerant of non-Sunday-goers. To focus on the fact that only some eleven per cent of Catholics go to Mass on a Sunday is to forget that Catholic values and Catholic social teaching run through the veins of very many more Catholics, and this is especially true of Catholics in public life.

I have never believed in wearing religion on my sleeve in public life. If anything, I am more likely to keep my rosary beads in my hip pocket. I appreciate that others may not practise their religion in the manner that I do – even if we are coreligionists. I think we have tagged a lot of people as lapsed Catholics when in fact they have not lost their faith. This is particularly the case in public life. It is also relevant to our reflections on Glynn. No doubt some Catholics, in his day, would not have thanked him for some of his actions. Some would have thought he had lost his way. As the only Catholic in the Hughes Ministry, he would probably have been tagged as a deserter by many Catholics.

Glynn lived in more sectarian times than we do now. Sectarianism remained a feature of Australian society until the 1960s. I can remember a clear divide between Catholics and Protestants in my youth. My uncle happened to be our parish priest. I know that he did not approve of such things as my participating in a football mate's wedding – he made it abundantly clear that I, or any Catholic boy, could not be part of the wedding party in an Anglican or other Christian church service. This has all quite changed now, but I remember growing up at the end of the sectarian era in which Glynn lived. How much more difficult must this have been in the 1890s? In such sectarian times, it was not only a fact that Glynn was the only Catholic in the Hughes Ministry, but it was also a fact that this would not have gone unnoticed. I can only imagine the difficulties he must have experienced in expressing Catholic values.

When he moved to Kapunda, only one in eight people in South Australia were Catholic, and prejudices were rife. Glynn experienced this quite brutally at the ballot box, when he was voted out of office. This appears to have taught him a lesson in humility, and I admire him very much for that. Come what may, I think he saw that it was important to be in the room. He saw that it was important to be tolerant and understanding; that it was better to engage.

When I look back at Glynn's life, I am easily convinced that he never lost his moral compass. This is telling for Catholics in public life today. We need to maintain our moral compass. We need to be tolerant and understanding, and to engage with those who disagree with us. Like Glynn, we also need to stand ready to express criticism of the church when this is justified. So he provides a model, but it is a complex one – not the model of the 'prominent Catholic'.

Although Glynn engaged in the federation debates with relish, it is a fact that whenever he did so, he would have encountered a hostile environment in most of the rooms that he walked into.

It was a time when there was a real fear of Irish Catholics – for political as well as religious reasons – and I admire the way in which he struck a path through such hostilities. It helped that he was no Irish maverick. Glynn was probably more liberal than conservative, and he was certainly capable of seeing value on all sides of politics. He demonstrated a steadfast loyalty to the British Empire despite supporting Irish independence. Again, I admire the sense in which he never advocated the Irish cause at the expense of Britain. This required a unique suppleness of mind, and this no doubt helped him to earn the respect of others.

There is an interesting parallel in his approach to federation. He believed in a form of federalism that did not exclude the rights of the States, just as he believed in Irish independence that did not undermine the British Empire. This is unusual, and I am particularly well placed to appreciate it, having seen the matter from both sides: as a State premier, I went to Canberra seeking the best deal for New South Wales; as federal Minister for Finance, I saw the other side of the coin.

Glynn touched and influenced a range of great debates, not only in relation to Federation, but also those such as the management of the Murray-Darling river system – an issue that remains of massive significance. He was influential in these debates because his approach allowed for outcomes based on compromise. He was always prepared to do the research in preparing an argument. He didn't think that you could win an argument simply by speaking loudly or often. He didn't rely upon the three-word slogans of today's politicians. Rather, he provided a meticulously argued case for his position; one that might involve going back centuries to draw on the lessons of history. He was able to produce the evidence, and this is what made him convincing. I would say that he was more of a negotiator than a litigator; one who believed that he could obtain negotiated outcomes because of his tenacity and commitment to reason.

Glynn's approach is particularly interesting in light of current debates about the Ramsay Centre for Western Civilisation. He was as committed to Western civilisation as one can be. The point is, however, that the commitment is not found in his repeatedly saying how good the West is, but in the very way he lived his life and conducted debates, which were littered with references to the Western canon.

Deakin regarded Glynn as a 'principled politician', and he was a man of principle who would prefer to decline an invitation to serve as Attorney-General rather than sit in a cabinet whose policies he could not support. This is in marked contrast to so-called 'Independents' today, who do not seem to have qualms about compromising themselves by accepting preferment. On the other hand, he was also prepared to engage with those with whom he disagreed. That said, not all his contemporaries shared Deakin's assessment. It seems that some resented his capacity to argue in a logical, well-reasoned fashion after having first done his homework. I would suggest that this was because many of his contemporaries were content to 'shoot from the hip' – as all too many politicians are today. Even from this distance, I can see, however, that his detailed arguments would have overwhelmed many in his audience. So it would not surprise me that he was not always a commanding orator on public occasions.

We Australians are good at meeting a challenge and moving on, living in the present, and rarely reflecting on the past. And yet the lessons of the past frequently clarify the challenges of the present. Henderson's essay captures one important but neglected instance of this. Glynn was by no means the standout of the Founding Fathers. An understanding of his approach to the challenges of his time is, however, instructive for us as we face today's challenges. Henderson's researches into Glynn's life and times demonstrate that if we knew more about the characters, intellects, motivations, and diverse views expressed as our Founding Fathers were shaping our great nation, today's challenges may not seem so insurmountable. Her brief portrayal of this Catholic Founding Father hopefully will inspire others to dig deeper and inform our twenty-first-century citizens about why we are who we are.

Glynn came to Australia because he couldn't make a living in Dublin. He came to Melbourne with all the right introductions, but he received no assistance. He was not enamoured of the place, and yet what becomes clear is that, as time went on, he wanted to be here. In a way, I can appreciate this experience. Both of my parents came here independently at the height of the Depression. So I know something of what it was like to come to Australia in search of prosperity. Like my own family, although Glynn came only to improve himself, he became so entrenched that he became committed to making a better Australia. I feel that I went into parliament for the sorts of reasons that Glynn did – because I could give more to society by doing so. It is not for me to weigh up the relative success that the two of us enjoyed in public life. What is so unusual about Glynn, however, is that he just happened to resolve to go into public life at the moment in history when this nation was birthing. It is a far better child today for Patrick McMahon Glynn's adroit midwifery.

Contributors

Peter Boyce AO is an adjunct professor at the University of Tasmania, having previously held the chair of political science at the Universities of Queensland and Western Australia, before serving for eleven years as vice-chancellor of Murdoch University.

John Fahey AC is the chancellor of Australian Catholic University, having previously served as the 38th premier of New South Wales and federal Minister for Finance in the First and Second Howard Ministries (1996-2001).

Damien Freeman is a fellow of the PM Glynn Institute at Australian Catholic University and editor of the Kapunda Press.

Anne Henderson AM is the deputy director of the Sydney Institute and a visiting fellow of the PM Glynn Institute.

Patrick Mullins is an adjunct assistant professor at the Centre for Creative and Cultural Research at the University of Canberra.

Suzanne D. Rutland OAM is an emeritus professor in the Department of Hebrew, Biblical and Jewish Studies at the University of Sydney.

Anne Twomey is a professor of constitutional law and director of the Constitutional Reform Unit at the University of Sydney.

Notes

Federation's man of letters, Anne Henderson

1 G. G. O'Collins, *Patrick McMahon Glynn: A Founder of Australian Federation* (Melbourne University Press, 1965), p. 87. Hereafter cited as *PMG: Founder of Federation*.

2 H. Whitington, "Patrick McMahon Glynn, KC, 1855/1931: a further character from Kerwin Maegraith's court sketchbook", *Law Society Bulletin*, Vol. 8, no. 11, Dec 1986, p. 339.

3 *PMG: Founder of Federation*, p. 87.

4 R. Garran, *Prosper the Commonwealth*, (Angus and Robertson, 1958), p. 113.

5 M. O'Collins, "Larrikins and apron strings", *The Age*, 8 April 1992.

6 Diaries of Patrick McMahon Glynn, 4 September 1880, pp. 1-2. Hereafter cited as Diaries of PMG. The diaries are held in the National Library of Australia, and may be viewed online at <https://nla.gov.au/nla.obj-572477534/view>.

7 Commonwealth, *Hansard*, House of Representatives, 17 August 1905, p. 1125.

8 *The Manifesto of the South Australian Land Nationalization Society* may be viewed online at <http://nzetc.victoria.ac.nz/tm/scholarly/tei-Stout82-t29-body-d1.html>.

9 P. M. Glynn, "Irish Intellectual Giants", *Austral Light*, 1 February 1913.

10 *The Advertiser*, 16 November 1897, p. 5.

11 G. G. O'Collins (ed.), *Patrick McMahon Glynn: Letters To His Family (1874-1927)* (Polding Press, 1974), p. 94. Hereafter cited as *PMG Letters*.

12 *Ibid.*, p. 56.

13 A. Deakin, *The Federal Story* (Melbourne University Press, 1963), p. 61.

14 R. Garran, *op. cit.*, p. 113.

15 Diaries of PMG, 1880, p. 47.

16 *PMG Letters*, p. 20.

17 Diaries of PMG, 1880, pp. 49-50.

18 *PMG: Founder of Federation*, pp. 23-24.

19 Diaries of PMG, 1881, p. 136.

20 *Ibid.*, p. 146.

21 *Ibid.*, p. 140.

22 *PMG Letters*, p. 54.

23 *PMG: Founder of Federation*, p. 40.

24 Diaries of PMG, 1883, p. 168.

25 Editorial, *Kapunda Herald*, 22 July 1890, p. 2.

26 H. Ergas, *The Australian*, 4 January 2019.

27 *PMG Letters*, p. 65.

28 *PMG: Founder of Federation*, pp. 38-39.

29 *PMG Letters*, p. 65.

30 *PMG: Founder of Federation*, p. 45.

31 Diaries of PMG, 1884, p. 250.

32 "The time may be right for land-value taxes", *The Economist*, 9 August 2018.

33 *PMG Letters*, p. 79.

34 *Ibid.*

35 *Ibid.*

36 *PMG Letters*, p. 108.

37 *Ibid.*

38 *Ibid.*

39 *Ibid.*, p. 121.

40 *Ibid.*, p. 131.

41 *Kapunda Herald*, 29 April 1890, p. 2.

42 *Kapunda Herald*, 25 April 1890, p. 2.

43 *PMG Letters*, p. 135.

44 *The Advertiser*, 16 November 1897, p. 5.

45 *PMG Letters*, p. 147.

46 *Official Report of the National Australasian Convention Debates*, Adelaide, 22 April 1897, p. 1184.

47 *Ibid.*

48 Interview with Fr Gerald O'Collins by Anne Henderson – Melbourne, 17 January 2019.

49 *The Advertiser*, 3 May 1895, p. 6.

50 *PMG: Founder of Federation*, p. 109.

51 H. Irving, *To Constitute a Nation: A Cultural History of Australia's Constitution* (Cambridge University Press, 1997), p. 3.

52 *Ibid.*, p. 4.

53 See: <http://www.naa.gov.au/collection/explore/federation/constitution-website/stories/quick-steps/pods/constitutional-convention-1897/index.html>.

54 Deakin, *op. cit.*, p. 74.

55 *The Argus*, 23 March 1897, p. 5.

56 *Daily Telegraph*, 25 March 1897, pp. 5-6.

57 *Convention Debates*, Adelaide, 22 April 1897, pp. 1184-6.

58 *Ibid.*

59 *Ibid.*

60 *Ibid.*

61 A. Atkinson, *The Europeans in Australia* (UNSW Press, 2014), Vol. 3, p. 268.

62 C. Bergmann, "'The Spirit of Religion': Australia's Constitutional Recognition of God in the Federal Convention Speeches of Patrick McMahon Glynn, 1897-98", BA (Hons) thesis, Monash University, October 2016, Chapter 1.

63 *Ibid.*

64 F. Brennan, "A History of Respectful Debate" in D. Freeman (ed.), *Today's Tyrants: Responding to Dyson Heydon* (Kapunda Press, 2018), p. 24.

65 *PMG: Founder of Federation*, p. 139.

66 *Convention Debates*, Melbourne, 1898, pp. 1732-33.

67 Brennan, *op. cit.*, p. 27.

68 *Convention Debates*, Melbourne, 1898.

69 G. Craven, "Taking a Legal Leap of Faith", *The Australian*, 5 January 2019.

70 *PMG Letters*, p. 160.

71 *PMG: Founder of Federation*, p. 122.

72 Diaries of PMG, 1899, p. 55.

73 *PMG Letters*, p. 184.

74 Commonwealth, *Hansard*, House of Representatives, 6 June 1903.

75 *Kapunda Herald*, 24 March 1885, p. 2.

76 *PMG: Founder of Federation*, p. 155.

77 See: <https://parlinfo.aph.gov.au/parlInfo/genpdf/hansard80/hansardr 80/1903-08-25/0020/hansard_frag.pdf;fileType=application%2Fpdf>.

78 *Ibid.*

79 See: <https://parlinfo.aph.gov.au/parlInfo/genpdf/hansard80/hansardr80/1911-09-07/0027/hansard_frag.pdf;fileType=application%2Fpdf>.

80 See: <https://parlinfo.aph.gov.au/parlInfo/genpdf/hansard80/hansardr80/ 1904-10-05/0010/hansard_frag.pdf;fileType=application%2Fpdf>.

81 P. M. Glynn, "An Explanation of the Bill", *The Advertiser*, 18 April 1898, p. 6.

82 *Convention Debates*, Melbourne, 1898, pp. 32-33.

83 *Ibid.*, p. 45.

84 *Ibid.*, p. 49.

85 *Ibid.*

86 *Ibid.*, p. 50.

87 *Ibid.*, p. 51.

88 *Ibid.*, p. 52.

89 D. Garden, "The Federation Drought of 1895-1903, El Niño and Society in Australia" in *Common Ground: Integrating the Social and Environmental in History* (Cambridge Scholars Publishing, 2010).

90 Commonwealth, *Hansard*, House of Representatives, 28 July 1904.

91 *PMG: Founder of Federation*, p. 218.

92 *The Advertiser*, 7 June 1915, p. 8.

93 *The Argus*, 22 July 1910, p. 4.

94 Commonwealth, *Hansard*, House of Representatives, 21 July 1910.

95 Commonwealth, *Hansard*, House of Representatives, 17 August 1905.

96 *PMG: Founder of Federation*, p. 245.

97 *PMG Letters*, p. 188.

98 The Honourable Hugh Mahon to Father Aphonsus Coen, 25 October 1916. National Library of Australia MS 4653, Series 18, Subseries 18.2.

99 G. Henderson, "The Deportation of Charles Jerger", *Labour History*, No. 31, November, 1976, pp. 61-78.

100 *Sydney Morning Herald,* 11 March 1918, p. 8.

101 The Honourable P. McMahon Glynn to the Honourable G. F. Pearce, 26 March 1918. National Library of Australia MS 4653, Series 18, Subseries 18.2.

102 G. Pearce to P. M. Glynn, 4 April 1918. *Ibid.*

103 P. M. Glynn to G. Pearce, 12 April 1918. *Ibid.*

104 G. Pearce to P. M. Glynn, 24 April 1918. *Ibid.*

105 P. M. Glynn to the Reverend Father Henry, 13 September 1918. *Ibid.*

106 P. M. Glynn to the Reverend Peter O'Reilly, 21 February 1919. *Ibid.*

107 P. M. Glynn to the Reverend Callistus Henry, 3 July 1919. *Ibid.*

108 Henderson, *op. cit.*, p. 69.

109 P. M. Glynn to C. Henry, 5 May 1920. *Supra.*

110 *Southern Cross*, 13 August 1920, p. 11.

111 P. M. Glynn, "The Death of a Century" in *The Southern Cross*. National Library of Australia MS 4653, Series 18.

112 Atkinson, *op. cit.*, p. 268.

113 Garran, *op. cit.*, p. 113.

114 Deakin, *op. cit.*, p. 90.

115 *Convention Debates*, Adelaide, 24 March 1897, p. 73.

116 P. M. Glynn, National Library of Australia MS 4653, Series 7.

117 Bergmann, *op. cit.*, Conclusion.

The biographer's tracks, Patrick Mullins

1 "An affable pretense," Bernard Crick writes, of statements of what is in a subject's mind: see B. Crick, *George Orwell: a life* (Secker & Warburg, 1980), p. *xxiii*.

2 V. Woolf, "The art of biography", *Death of the Moth and other essays* (University of Adelaide, 2015 [1942]).

3 G. Bolton, "The art of Australian political biography" in T. Arklay, J. Nethercote, and J. Wanna (eds), *Australian Political Lives: Chronicling political careers and administrative histories*, (ANU E-Press, 2006), p. 1.

4 E. H. Carr, *What is history?* (Penguin, 2008 [1961]), p. 45.

5 L. Edel, *Writing Lives: Principia Biographica* (Norton, 1984), pp. 13–14.

6 B. Pimlott, "The future of political biography", *Political Quarterly*, vol. 61, no. 2, 1990, p. 215.

7 L. Strachey, *Eminent Victorians* (Chatto & Windus, 1918), p. *ix*.

8 *Ibid.*, pp. ix–x.

Lawyer, Catholic and liberal conservative, Anne Twomey

1 G. G. O'Collins, *Patrick McMahon Glynn: A Founder of Australian Federation* (Melbourne University Press, 1965), pp. 135-6. Hereafter cited as *PMG: Founder of Federation.*

2 See, e.g., Glynn's maiden speech in the Commonwealth Parliament, raising the need for the Commonwealth to take over the Northern Territory of South Australia: Commonwealth, *Hansard,* House of Representatives, 22 May 1901, pp. 200-1. See also his pivotal role in ensuring the surrender of the Northern Territory to the Commonwealth: *PMG: Founder of Federation*, p. 200.

3 "Banquet to Messrs Coles and Glynn", *Adelaide Observer,* 8 March 1890, p. 34.

4 "Mr Glynn in Explanation", *Southern Cross* (Adelaide), 9 August 1895, p. 8. See also: *PMG: Founder of Federation*, pp. 75-78.

5 "The North Adelaide Election", *The Advertiser* (Adelaide), 31 May 1895, p. 6.

6 "Mr Glynn in Explanation", *Southern Cross* (Adelaide), 9 August 1895, p. 8. See also: *PMG: Founder of Federation*, pp. 75-78.

7 Note that at that time there was no compulsory voting, but the franchise had at least been expanded to include women.

8 *PMG: Founder of Federation*, p. 113.

9 *Ibid.*, p. 151.

10 "Address by Mr Glynn", *South Australian Register,* 8 April 1899, p. 5.

11 *PMG: Founder of Federation*, p. 152.

12 *Ibid.*, pp. 152-3.

13 S. Magarey (ed.), *Ever Yours, C H Spence—Catherine Helen Spence: An Autobiography* (Wakefield Press, 2005), p. 181.

14 *Official Report of the National Australasian Convention Debates,* Adelaide, 15 April 1897, p. 721.

15 *Convention Debates*, Adelaide, 22 April 1897, p. 1184.

16 *Ibid.*, p. 1186.

17 *Convention Debates*, Melbourne, 2 March 1898, p. 1737.

18 *Ibid.*, p. 1732.

19 *Ibid.*, p. 1733.

20 *Ibid.*

21 *Ibid.*

22 *Ibid.*, p. 1734.

23 *Ibid.*, p. 1740.

24 *Ibid.*

25 Western Australia is missing because it had not yet agreed to join the federation by the date that the Act was passed by the Westminster Parliament.

26 Commonwealth, *Hansard,* House of Representatives, 21 July 1910, p. 607.

27 *Ibid.*

28 *Ibid.*, pp. 624-5.

29 Note the current debate about whether such declarations and oaths should be altered before the next reign: R. Hazell and B. Morris, "Swearing in the New King: The Accession Declarations and Coronation Oaths", Constitution Unit, UCL, May 2018: <https://www.ucl.ac.uk/constitution-unit/sites/constitution-unit/files/180_swearing_in_the_new_king.pdf>.

30 From 1871, the Catholic Church forbade Catholics from attending Trinity College without special permission, as it was a Protestant institution. It is not clear whether Glynn obtained permission to do so. In later times, Catholics were excommunicated for attending Trinity College, a rule that was only lifted in 1970: "Irish Catholic Church Lifts Trinity College Ban", *New York Times,* 28 June 1970.

31 Note his written opinions as Attorney-General on a wide range of subjects in: P. Brazil (ed.), *Opinions of Attorneys-General of the Commonwealth of Australia* (AGPS, 1981), Vol. I: 1901-14, pp. 429-484.

32 *Convention Debates*, Adelaide, 24 March 1897, pp. 70-71.

33 Commonwealth, *Hansard,* House of Representatives, 22 May 1901, pp. 199-200; and 29 May 1901, p. 390.

34 "High Court Bench – Mr Glynn's Name Mentioned", *Sydney Morning Herald*, 25 November 1912, p. 10.

35 *PMG: Founder of Federation*, p. 234.

36 "High Court – Mr Glynn a Certainty", *Sydney Morning Herald,* 13 December 1912, p. 8.

37 "The High Court – Mr Duffy Appointed", *The Register* (Adelaide), 6 February 1913, p. 7.

38 "The High Court Bench – Mr Glynn Overlooked – Disappointment in Adelaide", *The Sun* (Sydney), 6 February 1913, p. 7.

39 T. Simpson, "Appointments that Might Have Been" in T. Blackshield, M. Coper and G. Williams (eds), *The Oxford Companion to the High Court of Australia* (Oxford University Press, 2001), p. 24.

40 "Death of the Hon P McMahon Glynn", *The Catholic Press* (Sydney), 5 November 1931, p. 19; "The Whispering Gallery", *Punch* (Melbourne), 13 February 1913, p. 7; *PMG: Founder of Federation*, p. 234.

41 "The Whispering Gallery", *Punch* (Melbourne), 20 February 1913, p. 7.

42 "New High Court Judge – Mr Glynn mentioned for appointment", *The Recorder* (Port Pirie, SA), 12 January 1920, p. 1.

Personality and Prejudice: Glynn and Isaacs compared, Suzanne D. Rutland

1 Z. Cowen, "Isaacs, Sir Isaac Alfred (1855-1948)", *Australian Dictionary of Biography*, National Centre of Biography, Australian National University, <http://adb.anu.edu.au/biography/isaacs-sir-isaac-alfred-6805/text11773>, published first in hardcopy in 1983, accessed online 29 April 2019.

2 As quoted in Z. Cowen, *Isaac Isaacs* (University of Queensland Press, 1967, 1993), p. 98.

3 F. Fletcher, "The Victorian Jewish Community, 1891–1901: Its Inter-relationship with the Majority Gentile Community", *Australian Jewish Historical Society Journal*, vol. 13, no. 5, 1978.

4 Cited in *Ibid.*, p. 250.

5 H. Rubinstein, *The Jews in Australia: A Thematic History*, Volume I, 1788-1945 (Heinemann, 1991), pp. 46-76.

6 C. Tatz, *A Course of History; Monash Country Club, 1931-2001* (Allen & Unwin, 2002), p. 34.

7 For a more detailed discussion of Jews and Federation, see H. H. Glass, "Some Jews and the Federal Movement", *Australian Jewish Historical Society Journal*, vol. 3, no. 6, 1951 and M. Z. Forbes, "The Federation of the Commonwealth and the Role of Australian Jews", *Australian Jewish Historical Society Journal*, Vol. 15, no. 4, 2001, pp. 506–46.

8 Cowen, *Isaac Isaacs*, p. 99.

9 Cited in L. Fredman, "Isaacs in Politics", *Australian Jewish Historical Society Journal*, vol. 5, no. 4, 1961, pp. 189–203.

10 Cowen, *Isaac Isaacs*, p. 57.

11 *Ibid.*

12 M. Gordon, *Sir Isaac Isaacs: A Life of Service* (Heinemann, 1963), p. 79.

13 Cowen, *Isaac Isaacs*, p. 84.

14 *Ibid.*, pp. 84-5.

15 *The Maccabean*, 26 April 1929.

16 See S. D. Rutland, *Edge of the Diaspora: Two Centuries of Jewish Settlement in Australia* (Brandl & Schlesinger, 2001, p. 171.

17 Cowen, *Isaac Isaacs*, p.232.

18 *Hebrew Standard of Australasia*, 20 November 1941.

19 S. D. Rutland, *Pages of History: A Century of the Australian Jewish Press* (Australian Jewish Press, 1995), pp. 93-95.

20 C. Tatz, *A Course of History: Monash Country Club, 1931-2001* (Allen & Unwin, 2002), p. 28.

Index